DOING GOD'S WILL: USING CHRISTIAN FAITH AND PSYCHOLOGY

James Battle, Ph.D.

James Battle and Associates Ltd.
Suite 1102 10235 124 Street
Edmonton, AB
T5N 1P6

International Standard Book Number: 978-0-9683443-7-8

Registration Number: 1045747

Canadian Cataloguing in Publication Data

Battle, James
Doing God's Will: Using Christian Faith and Psychology
Includes Bibliographical references.

1. Christian Faith Psychology   2. Commitment and Peace

TABLE OF CONTENTS

PART V   177

THEN I REFLECTED AND THANKED MY GOD

I remember the day my mother died
I didn't shed a tear, but I cried
Then I reflected and thanked my God
I remember the trying adolescent years
The many uncertainties and fears
Then I reflected and thanked my God
I remember when I first ventured from home
Cast away in a world all alone
Then I reflected and thanked my God
I remember becoming a man tall and strong
The many problems I had trying to sort right from wrong
Then I reflected and thanked my God
I remember the day I took a wife to share my dreams
The happiness we found near brooks and streams
Then I reflected and thanked my God
I remember the days our children were born
When we celebrated with flute and horn
Then I reflected and thanked my God
I remember all the blessings I received
Simply because I loved and believed
Then I reflected and thanked my God
I remember I pledged to do thy will
Until my body is peaceful and still
Then I reflected and thanked my God.

James Battle (1997)

ACKNOWLEDGEMENTS

THE WRITER GRATEFULLY ACKNOWLEDGES the support of the individuals who contributed to the development and publication of this book. First, I wish to recognize the many students and clients who provided me the opportunities to interact with them, develop, and test the strategies described in this book, that have proven to be effective in assisting users in achieving desired results.

Second, I thank my daughter Christina, son Jamie, and friend Don Adams for their dedication and support and the many hours they put in typing the book.

Third, I thank Don Adams and Barbara Stratichuk for the excellent job they did typesetting the manuscript.

Fourth, I thank my very good friends Hugh Ross, Herb Dobbins, and Harold Woods for conducting searches of the Christian Bible and providing insights.

Fifth, I thank my family, Dorothy, Christina, and Jamie, for their unconditional love and the assistance, co-operation, support and care they provided me during the term of this project and over the years.

Sixth, I thank my mother-in-law Edith Cary for being the elder of our extended family and for persevering and doing God's will in spite of the behavior of others.

Finally, I dedicate this publication to all peoples who strive to live in harmony and make our world a better place for all.

IN MEMORY

THIS BOOK IS DEDICATED IN MEMORY OF my wife's mother, Edith Cary who was my real superstar. She provided me and my family; Dorothy, Christina, and Jamie unconditional love, support, respect and encouragement. Edith, as she was referred to by those who knew her, was an authentic Christian, called by God to do His will. She died on November 5, 2006.

Edith was a loving mother, grandmother, and great grandmother who dedicated her life to serving others and doing God's will. My mother-law was the kind of person who provided individuals at all levels of development respect and exerted positive effects on all those that she served.

My wife's mother loved children. She passed this disposition to my wife, and they both inspired me to write the following poem:

CHILDREN: IMPORTANT RESOURCES

I have learned during my brief life
That things worthwhile require sacrifice
Children are worthy, capable, and significant:
With proper love and nurturance,
They will grow up to be magnificent.
Children may be simple, complex, weak or strong.
Their behavior may be shy, aggressive, right or wrong,
Children are the most important sources of worth and life:
They are worthy of the love of mom, dad, husband and wife
How parents handle children, determines what they will be,
How they see life, the world, you and me.
Children's emotions are strong and true.
Teach them to love themselves, and they will love you.

James Battle

I esteem Mrs. Cary very highly and thank God for providing me the opportunity to be her son-in-law. My mother-in-law was a kind, friendly, warm hearted, generous person who provided all people respect. She inspired me to write this book and the following poem I call "Gramma:"

GRAMMA

Gramma is the one who
made the greatest sacrifice
By giving me unconditional love and life.
Gramma made it clear so that I could see
The kind of person that I should be.
Gramma taught me how to work and plan
to respect you and my fellow man.
Gramma's wisdom is faith based and genuine
The kind of knowledge that lasts a life time.
Gramma is always available to lend a hand
to her children, family and fellow man.
Gramma will continue to be
the real superstar who
provided unconditional love,
respect and encouragement for me
I thank you Gramma
for everything that I am
and will be
How I see life, the world,
you and me.

James Battle

PREFACE

ALTHOUGH MANY BOOKS HAVE BEEN written about Christianity, few have addressed the relationship between Christian faith and psychology. In this book, we provide insights regarding the roles that Christian faith and psychology have played and continue to play in the lives of humans.

This book is organized into nine parts.

PART I provides an introduction to the text and document historical information regarding the origins of the Christian faith and psychology. Also, in this part, we show the relationship between psychology and the Christian faith and offer insights regarding how tenets of both psychology and the Christian faith influence human behavior.

PART II provides insights regarding the effects that beliefs and perceptions exert on human behavior. Also, in this part we describe a psychotherapeutic approach that have demonstrated effectiveness in helping patients and clients experiencing a wide variety of problems and conclude that leaders of Christian churches and psychotherapists as well provide those that they serve insights and interact with them in fashions that are similar. In addition, in this part, we provide an overview of the construct of self-esteem and support the position which assumes that emphasizing the enhancement of self-esteem is in concert with the tenets of the Christian faith. In this part, the importance of self-esteem is emphasized and we describe strategies that have demonstrated effectiveness in enhancing perception of self-worth. This part also, offers information regarding the need for supporters of the Christian faith to provide mission and service.

PART III provides information that individuals can use in their efforts to comply with God's commandments and the demands of their environments. This part lists and describes tools that supporters of the Christian faith and others can use to obtain personal goals and achieve desired levels of success. Also, this part shows readers how to use cognitive strategies to achieve problem resolution and help them maintain and strengthen their Christian faith. This part emphasizes the need to provide mutual respect and encouragement to others while interacting with them and offer readers the opportunity to assess their own levels of both constructs.

PART IV provides insights derived from tenets of the Christian faith and show readers how they can serve God and do His will. In this part, the importance of being authentic Christians is emphasized and positions based on faith that individuals can use to promote authentic Christian values are documented. In addition, this part provides statements of faith inspired from Christian tenets and knowledge derived from the discipline of psychology that have been employed by humans over the years and continue to be relevant for those residing in contemporary societies.

PART V provides concluding remarks to the book.

PART VI provides an overview of the author's views regarding the importance of service and mission.

PART VII provides a glossary of terms and references to the book.

PART VIII provides an annotated list of recommended readings and resource materials.

PART IX provides the epilogue to the book.

INTRODUCTION

CHRISTIAN FAITH AND PSYCHOLOGY have existed over the ages and exerted powerful influences on the lives of humans of every generation.

Although it is common for countries to have in place policies promoting the separation of religion and State, religious beliefs continue to affect the contributions of philosophers, artists, educators, clinicians, and scientists. Beliefs exert insidious, persistent, powerful effects on how humans think and behave.

Using psychology to do God's will is not restricted to the professionally trained psychologist; rather individuals performing a wide spectrum of roles can employ tenets of psychology to assist them in doing God's will. Also, individuals at all developmental stages ranging from early childhood to advanced adulthood can incorporate psychological strategies in their daily routine to help them achieve the desired result of doing God's will.

The knowledge incorporated in this text is both empirically and spiritually inspired; it is derived from scientific research and tenets of the Christian religion.

Enlightened Christian psychologists encourage the individuals they serve to behave in fashions that are consistent with the final seven of God's commandments. Those who are both enlightened and authentic Christian psychologists encourage their patients and clients to incorporate all Ten Commandments into their daily routine.

Although most psychologists are not ordained ministers they are important resources that can promote the display of behavior that is in concert with Christian beliefs and values.

In Hebrews 10: 5 -10, Christ said: "See, I have come to do Your will…"

In the book, I provide effective knowledge and encourage readers at all developmental levels to commit themselves to doing God's will.

This book represents my efforts to provide effective knowledge and contribute to the well being of all peoples in our world community and to promote mutual respect, harmony and peaceful interactions among members of our human group.

PART I

Background Information

CHAPTER 1

CHRISTIAN FAITH AND PSYCHOLOGY

IN THIS CHAPTER WE PROVIDE HISTORICAL information regarding the origins of the Christian faith and psychology.

CHRISTIAN FAITH

The beginning of the Christian faith can be traced to 33 AD when Jesus Christ, the Son of God commissioned the establishment of the Roman Catholic Church. The Catholic faith, which is based on the premise of openness to the world has endured the test of time and continues to be among the most prominent Christian religions today. Other prominent Christian denominations include:

Lutherans

The Lutherans that were introduced by Martin Luther in 1517 is the world's largest protestant denomination.

Presbyterians

The Presbyterians is a protestant denomination that was founded by John Calvin in 1560.

Episcopalians

The Episcopalian church commonly referred to, as The Church of England or The Anglican Church is a protestant denomination that was started by Henry VIII in 1543.

Baptists

The Baptist is a protestant denomination that was formed by a small group of English dissenters in 1607.

United

The United is a protestant denomination that was founded by Theophilus in the 1500's.

Quakers

The Quakers is a protestant denomination founded by George Fox in the 1600's when he emphasized the importance of personal experience of the light of God's Holy Spirit.

Methodists

The Methodist Church is a protestant denomination that was founded by John and Charles Wesley in 1744.

Christian Science

The Christian Science Church is a protestant denomination founded by Mary Baker Eddy in 1879.

Jehovah Witnesses

The Jehovah Witnesses Church is a protestant denomination founded by Charles Taze Russell in 1872.

Pentecostals

The roots of the Pentecostal denomination can be traced to John Wesley in 1901

Although there are differences among Christian denominations, the similarities outweigh the differences;

all Christian denominations recognize God, and His son Jesus Christ and view them as being the base and foundation of the Christian faith.

PSYCHOLOGY

Psychology, like the Christian faith has endured the test of time and continues to be relevant.

The Greek Theophrastus (372-287 B.C.) was one of the first contributors in the field of psychology. He was followed by other noteworthy contributors including:

Galen (A.D. 130-200) who developed a procedure for describing personality and identifying character types.

Hippocrates (460-367 B.C.) who proposed four body humors that correspond to character types.

Phillipe Pinel (1745-1826) who is generally credited with being the first therapist to remove the chains of mentally ill patients.

Wilheim Wundt (1832-1920) who established the first psychological laboratory in Leipzig Germany in 1879.

Alfred Binet (1852-1911) who developed the first intelligence test in 1905.

Sigmund Freud (1856-1939) who provided the first comprehensive theory of personality.

A problem of early contributors to both the Christian faith and psychology was that of demonistic possession. Members of the Christian faith who played prominent roles in the controversy were two German Dominican monks named Johann Sprenger, and Heinrich Kraemer. These spiritual leaders proposed that there were two types of demonistic possession:

Unwilling possession, a form in which the individual is possessed by the devil against his will. The possessed person was being punished by God for his sins, and

Willing possession, in which the individual being a faithful follower of satan, chose to be possessed.

Sprenger and Kraemer reserved the first category for mental patients and the latter for witches. Thus, they concerned themselves basically with the extermination of witches. Their major thesis was presented in the manuscript entitled, "Malleus Maleficarum", or "witches hammer." In this book, Sprenger and Kraemer confirmed the existence of witches, established means of identifying them and delineated the legal procedures for prosecuting and sentencing them. The propositions incorporated in the Malleus Maleficarum were accepted almost universally by Catholics and Protestants throughout the world for many years.

Sprenger and Kraemer, therefore, were instrumental in establishing the practice of witch hunting that prevailed for more than two hundred years, and resulted in the torture of hundreds of thousands of mentally ill men, women and children.

Sprenger and Kraemer's influence was so overwhelming that many scientifically trained men and respected physicians during this period accepted the propositions they proposed.

For instance, Ambroise Pare (1510-1590), a distinguished physician and pioneer in the field of surgery believed that demons caused women to become witches and that they should be destroyed, rather than treated as sick individuals.

I suspect that Sprenger and Kraemer employed the psychological defense mechanism reaction formation which involves the creation of a pattern of behavior which is directly opposite to how they truly felt. As monks, they verbalized love for humans, while concealing their hatred of women.

I am of the opinion that sinners are those individuals who have been provided authentic knowledge regarding God and His son Jesus Christ, but refuse to believe the information communicated and reject God and His son, Jesus Christ.

Satan, was created by God, but he became evil by his own doing. Thus, those individuals who disobey God, display evilness, envy, and reject God are sinners because of the behavior that they display. Sinners employ defense mechanisms in efforts to convince themselves and others that their behavior is not incongruent with Christian tenets.

PSYCHOLOGICAL DEFENSE MECHANISMS

The use of defense mechanisms represents an individual's unconscious attempts to rid him or herself of anxiety.

Although Freud was the first to provide the concept of defense mechanism, others (*e.g. Rogers and Adler*) made contributions in this area.

PSYCHOLOGICAL DEFENSES

1. Operate at an unconscious level

• The individual employing defenses does not know that he/she is utilizing them.

2. Individuals employ defense mechanisms to protect themselves from anxiety and guilt.

• The individual uses defenses to reduce threat.

3. The use of defenses indicates varying degrees of psychological or emotional disturbance.

• More frequent use of certain defenses indicates more serious degrees of adjustment problems.

4. All individuals use defense mechanisms.

- Perfection does not exist in personality.

Psychological defenses frequently employed by sinners are:

a) Projection

and

b) Rationalization.

PROJECTION

Projection is a defense in which the individual rids him or herself of threatening drives, impulses and needs by attributing them to others. Thus, the projecting individual attributes his own characteristics or impulses (usually always undesirable ones) to others. One can observe evidence of projection in our day to day interactions when we observe the individual who possesses hostile and aggressive impulses insisting that others are aggressive and inhumane; in the frightened child who insists that other children are cowards or chickens; in the student who blames his instructor for his poor grades; in the businessman who insists that he lost a sale because of the incompetence of his secretary; in the football player who projects the blame for losing a key game on his team-mates; in the baseball player who strikes out and attributes it to faulty footwear; and in the couple who separates and blames each other for the marriage failure. In each of the examples presented above the projecting individual reduced feelings of discomfort, guilt and anxiety by attributing blame for undesirable behavior to others.

RATIONALIZATION

Rationalization is a defense in which the individual provides a socially acceptable reason for his undesirable behavior. It provides the individual with an excuse which enables him to reduce threat by justifying his socially unacceptable actions to himself and others. The rationalizing individual makes excuses which convince him that his illogical, irrational behavior is not as ridiculous as it actually is.

Authentic Christians

Authentic Christians, unlike sinners are individuals who are committed to doing God's will. In the following statement, I offer my definition of the authentic Christian.

An authentic Christian is an individual who realizes that in the eyes of God we are all brothers and sisters of equal worth.

Authentic Christians recognize the inherent worth of each individual and do not emit behavior that impedes the development of others. Authentic Christians maintain steadfast, unswerving love for God, permit Him to work within them and realize that every "good thing" they produce is due to God working within them. Authentic Christians offer sincere speech, do not judge individuals that they are not mandated to assess, but provide genuine recognition for the behavior of self and others.

Christian Tenets and Constructs

The following are some important tenets and constructs:

- God is God of All

- God's son, Jesus Christ is Lord of all

- Holy Spirit is the force, source or mechanism that God employs to interact with his children

- God chooses some of his children for special assignments, to perform specific tasks

- All humans are brothers and sisters of equal worth

- Sin is behavior that God disapproves of

- Temptation: a desire to display an action

- Belief: something considered to be true

- Beliefs determine how humans interact with one another and the behavior they display

I encourage individuals to use the effective knowledge incorporated in this chapter to assist themselves in their efforts to achieve desired results.

SUMMARY

- Both Christian faith and psychology have existed over the ages and exerted strong influences

- Beliefs exert powerful effects on human behavior.

- Jesus Christ is the mainstay of the Christian faith.

- The Lutheran church is the world's largest protestant denomination.

- Both similarities and differences exist among all Christian denominations.

- Both psychology and the Christian faith have endured the test of time.

- The first psychological laboratory was established in Leipzig, Germany.

- The problem of demonistic possession confronted supporters of psychology and the Christian faith.

- Battle proposes that supporters of both psychology and the Christian faith employ psychological defense mechanisms.

- Sinners reject God and His son Jesus Christ.

- Freud, who developed the most comprehensive theory of personality, was the first to provide the concept of defense mechanisms.

- Battle proposes that authentic Christians recognize the inherent worth of all individuals.

PART II

Promoting Worth

And Christian Values

CHAPTER 2

BELIEF, WORTH, KNOWLEDGE AND BEHAVIOR

A BELIEF IS AN OPINION OR DISPOSITION THAT an individual possesses which he or she considers to be true. I summarize my personal belief in God in the following statement.

A PERSONAL BELIEF

I (Battle, 2006)

Believe:

That

1. My God is the only true God

That

2. My God is God of all creation

That

3. God's Son, Jesus Christ is the only true Lord

That

4. Jesus Christ is Lord of all humans

That

5. All humans are brothers and sisters of equal worth

In the following, I also share my opinion regarding God.

GOD WITHIN US

I am of the opinion that:

*God the creator of heaven and earth

Is the

*One, invisible, inscrutable

And only

*True God

When we have

*Faith in God

and permit Him to:

*Work within us

we

*Do good things

when we

*Reject God

and refuse to let Him

*work within us

we

*Sin

and produce

*Results that are Bad and Evil

I am of the opinion that "Effective" knowledge is the best medicine for psychological and relationship problems. The format of the Ten Commandments provides support for this position. The first three instruct humans to worship only the one true God, love him, maintain faith in Him and keep his commandments. The last seven commandments provide instructions regarding relations with others.

The strategies incorporated in this chapter and others that follow have demonstrated effectiveness in helping individuals obtain personal goals and achieve desired levels of success.

I recommend that individuals practice employing effective knowledge on a regular basis. I made this position clear on page fifteen of my book entitled "Strategies That You Can Use To Enhance Your Own Self-Esteem And Well Being" when I said:

> …When using the strategies we recommend in this book remember to practice them on a regular basis. Also, remember that practice makes improvement, not perfection as many individuals propose. Actually perfection does not exist in personality and for one to insist that she has to be perfect in order to be worthwhile is self-defeating…

Because of my beliefs, as a psychotherapist, I provide the individuals I serve homework assignments and expose them to an approach, I call Rational – Eclectic Therapy.

RATIONAL–ECLECTIC THERAPY

I utilize a modified version of Ellis' approach which I call the "Rational-Eclectic Approach" in my treatment of clients experiencing adjustment failures (*Battle, 1991*).

This approach is basically the same as Ellis' Rational-Emotive Approach, but we use aspects of other theoretical orientations (e.g. client-centered, socio-cultural, behavioral, psychoanalytic) that are less directive, place greater importance on the affects of early interactions between parent and child, on the acquisition of insight, and on the process of defense. The approach is comprised of the following steps:

Step 1.

Assessment and historical review: The patient is administered a number of personality inventories in an attempt to gather relevant data regarding his or her current modes of functioning. Patient expectations are assessed and therapeutic goals are established. A brief homework assignment is provided.

Step 2.

Interpretation of results: At this step, results earned on measures of personality are interpreted to the patient. A brief review of the major tenets of the rational-eclectic point of view is provided, and the patient is again provided a homework assignment.

Step 3.

Identification of irrational premises and self-defeating patterns: Irrational and illogical ideas possessed by the patient are identified, and the patient is shown why these ideas "don't' work well." Self-defeating patterns are identified. Again, the patient is given a homework assignment.

Step 4.

Exploration of irrational premises and self-defeating patterns: Irrational dispositions and self-defeating patterns are attacked directly, and the patient is made aware of the probable consequences of these actions. Again, there is homework for the patient.

Step 5.

Introduction of adaptive forms of behavior: Alternative modes of behavior are discussed, and the patient is shown how to function more effectively. Again, homework.

Step 6.

The client is given oral examinations in which the information taught during therapy sessions is reviewed. During the examinations the insights gained by the patient or client are identified and effective methods of thinking and behaving are delineated. Again, homework.

Step 7.

Rehearsal of newly acquired modes of behavior: The patient at this point practices responding in a more rational fashion under the guidance of the therapist in the therapeutic environment. More homework.

Step 8.

Generalization of newly acquired skills into the general social milieu: The patient is shown how to take the skills learned in therapy and apply them in the real world. As usual, there is homework.

Step 9.

Review and follow-up: A review of the progress that has been made in therapy and elsewhere is conducted. The patient is encouraged to continually practice the newly developed skills and to assign homework to himself as often as he feels it is needed.

Homework assignments in steps 1 and 2, basically involve readings in the area of rational-emotive psychotherapy; whereas subsequent homework assignments involve actual practice of rational tenets. For example, attempting to gain greater control over emotions, identifying self-defeating patterns and making a concerted effort to eliminate them, thinking in a more rational fashion and emitting behavior that is self-enhancing, rather then self-defeating.

Patients receiving "rational-eclectic therapy" are instructed to contact the therapist at weekly intervals for a three-week period immediately following the therapeutic sessions to discuss how they are functioning in their day-to-day activities. Having the patient contact the therapist serves a number of functions including:

a) It assists the patient in applying his newly acquired skills;

b) It provides feedback regarding how the patient is adjusting;

c) It impresses upon the patient that it is beneficial to continually strive towards gaining increasingly greater degrees of rationality;

d) It conveys to the patient that he is responsible for his own actions and is capable of (if he behaves rationally) emitting behavior that is self-enhancing.   *(Battle, 1983, pp. 541-542)*

The Eclectic Therapist uses techniques such as Reflective Listening in his or her attempts to assist the client in developing more positive perceptions of self-worth. The major role of the psychotherapist is to function as a teacher, specializing in the psychology of human dynamics.

As an effective teacher, the therapist communicates to his client that he possesses knowledge that he will give to his client. This knowledge, the therapist lets the client know, will assist him in perceiving more accurately and behaving more effectively. Thus, the therapist interacts with the patient or client in a fashion that enables that person to develop his potential most efficiently.

Eclectic Therapists

1. Instruct or teach their clients effective ways of perceiving.

2. Assist their clients in gaining greater insights regarding the etiology (or cause) of their behavior.

3. Teach their clients strategies for identifying and clarifying problem situations effectively.

4. Instruct their clients in modes of behaving that are self-enhancing rather than self-defeating.

5. Teach their clients effective strategies for exploring alternatives.

God provides all of His children unconditional love; popes, bishops, priests, pastors, and ministers provide members of their denominations unconditional positive regard. Psychologists who practice psychotherapy provide their patients and clients unconditional positive regard and interacts with them in a non-judgemental fashion. The therapist also encourages clients, and provides them mutual respect.

I am of the opinion that cognitive psychotherapy works best for both Christians and non-Christians as well. Some cognitive strategies that I employ while providing therapy for clients and patients are listed in the following:

COGNITIVE PSYCHOTHERAPY

Therapists who practice cognitive therapy teach clients and patients a variety of strategies including:

1. A-B-C Paradigm

The A-B-C Paradigm is a model which illustrates how the psychic system works and deals with thought, perception, feelings, and behavior.

2. Ten-Step Countdown Procedure

The Ten-Step Countdown is a cognitive procedure that one can use to impede the emission of impulsive behavior and increase the probability of displaying behavior that is self-enhancing rather than self-defeating.

3. Ten-Question Procedure

The Ten Question Procedure is a strategy that individuals can use to assist themselves in decision making and behaving in fashions that are self-enhancing.

4. Dot Focusing Cognitive Strategy

Dot Focusing is a strategy that one can use to control arousal and diminish symptoms of anxiety.

5. They Said

They Said is an inspirational statement that individuals can use in their efforts to overcome challenges, obtain goals and achieve success.

6. Reflective Listening

Reflective Listening is a cognitive strategy that individuals can use to achieve problem resolution.

7. Show Them

Show Them is a poem that incorporates stanzas of encouragement which individuals can use to motivate themselves to obtain personal goals and achieve desired levels of success.

8. Positive Action Strategies

Positive Action Strategies are time-tested ways of thinking and reacting that have demonstrated effectiveness in helping individuals obtain goals and emit behavior that is self-enhancing.

9. Effective Responses to "Put-Downs"

Effective Responses to "Put-Downs" is a document which describes how individuals can deal effectively with those who attempt to demean them by employing "put-downs."

PERCEPTION AND BEHAVIOR

The group of psychologists who identify themselves as being phenomenologists stress the importance of subjective perception and propose that the individual reacts to the world in terms of his or her perception of it. This position has endured the test of time extending centuries and continues to be relevant to humans currently residing on earth. Authentic Christians tend to perceive the world in a certain fashion and their perception determines the behavior they display. Bowman (1966) emphasized the important influence that perception has on behavior when he said:

"... It is generally assumed that the way a person

thinks of himself determines the general intent and direction of a person's behavior. In other words, persons who think of themselves negatively will behave in self-defeating ways, even though they may choose a variety of behavioral patterns in the process."

Perception is the major force compelling behavior. If a supporter of the Christian faith maintains the perception that he cannot succeed or accomplish desired results, he will not because this disposition often leads to a self-fulfilling prophecy which is characterized by a tendency to behave in a fashion that is in concert with previously established perceptions, and expectations. Because of this, it is important that Christians and others as well think positive and maintain the expectation that they will succeed. When they do this, they increase the probability of success. Thus, I encourage supporters of the Christian faith not to say, "if I succeed;" but rather say, "when I succeed."

Perceptions are similar to beliefs, but they differ. Conscious perception which compels behavior is derived from thought. Thoughts are similar to beliefs; however, they differ in that thought typically operates at an unconscious level, whereas beliefs generally operate at a conscious level. (Battle 1997, page 24, Overcoming Racism and Achieving Success)

As an authentic Christian, I encourage others to read the Ten Commandments, Apostle's Creed, and the Lord's Prayer on a regular basis:

THE TEN COMMANDMENTS

1. I am the Lord your God: you shall not have strange Gods before Me.

2. You shall not take the name of the Lord your God in vain.

3. Remember to keep holy the Lord's Day.

4. Honor your father and your mother.

5. You shall not kill.

6. You shall not commit adultery.

7. You shall not steal.

8. You shall not bear false witness against your neighbor.

9. You shall not covet your neighbor's wife.

10. You shall not covet your neighbor's goods.

APOSTLE'S CREED

I believe in God, the Father almighty,

Creator of heaven and earth.

I believe in Jesus Christ, his only Son, our Lord.

He was conceived by the power of the Holy Spirit

And born of the Virgin Mary.

He suffered under Pontius Pilate,

Was crucified, died, and was buried.

He descended to hell.

On the third day he rose again.

He ascended into heaven,

And is seated at the right hand of the Father.

He will come again to judge the living and the dead.

I believe in the Holy Spirit,

The holy catholic Church,

The communion of saints,

The forgiveness of sins,

The resurrection of the body,

And the life everlasting. Amen.

THE LORD'S PRAYER

Our Father, who art in heaven, hallowed be Thy name.

Thy kingdom come; Thy will be done on earth, as it is in heaven.

Give us this day, our daily bread, and forgive us our trespasses,

As we forgive those who trespass against us,

And lead us not into temptation, but deliver us from evil for,

Thine is the kingdom, and the power, and the glory, forever, and ever. Amen.

Reading God's fourth commandment:

"Honor your father and mother" inspired me to write the following poem to honor my mom and dad.

MY MOM AND DAD

Of all the people in my life,
My mom and dad made the greatest sacrifice.
My mom and dad were a wonderful pair,
Who provided me unconditional love, support
and care.
They made things clear to me so that I could see,
The positive things in you and me.
They taught me how to work and plan,
To think for myself and respect my fellowman.
I thank my parents for how I see,
My views of the world, life, you and me.

James Battle

HUMAN JEALOUSY

I, (*Battle, 2006*) propose that there are two types of jealousy. These are described in the following statement.

Two types of Jealousy

1. Love Jealousy

Jealousy that is compelled by caring.

2. Hate Jealousy

Jealousy that is compelled by the desire to hurt or injury.

The intent of hate jealousy is to:

Destroy a person who is perceived as being more talented and preferred by others.

Individuals displaying hate jealousy:

Utilize defensive manoeuvres in efforts to:

a) Diminish the worth of their victims.

Hate Jealousy: An example

Dr. James Battle and Associates Ltd., solely owned by my wife and I, hired an employee who was seeking employment to work as a receptionist/secretary. Shortly thereafter, the individual displayed behavior that my wife and I considered to be inappropriate, but we retained the person as an employee. However, as time passed, the individual's behavior became more self-centered and dictatorial. The final "straw" occurred when the individual refused to perform a role responsibility. When confronted the individual "stormed" out of our facility and quit working for us. When this happened, I predicted that the individual would display hate jealousy and attempt to convince others to work against me, and my wife. As predicted, approximately one week after the individual "stormed" out of our facility, a relative of the person phoned my wife and dis-invited my family to a previously scheduled supper. This action was intended to injure my wife and me. At the time of this writing which is more than twenty four months after the "storming out" incidence, the hate jealousy continues.

I, (J. Battle, 2006) propose that humans who display hate jealousy possess low or pseudo (inauthentic) self-esteem. Battle (1981, 1982, 1988, 1992, 1993, 1994) defined self-esteem in the following fashion:

...Self–esteem refers to the perception the individual possesses of his/her own worth. An individual's perception of self develops gradually and becomes more differentiated as he/she matures and interacts with significant others. Perception of self-worth, once established, tends to be fairly stable and resistant to change.

My views regarding the relationship between self-esteem and Christianity are recorded in the following statement taken from my book entitled "Misconceptions Regarding Self-Esteem".

MISCONCEPTION: EMPHASIS ON SELF-ESTEEM WEAKENS CHRISTIAN VALUES

It is clear to me that the interactive strategies I propose are in concert with the teaching of the Christian Bible. For example, I am of the opinion that mutual respect" is in concert with the biblical position of "love thou neighbor as thyself;" in the eyes of God we are all of equal worth and God's love for each of us is unconditional. The roots of self-esteem can be traced to the Holy Bible. For instance, the words of Christ, recorded in John 13:34 reads "A new commandment I give you, that you love one another." (Battle, 1990, page 9)

I am a Christian who believes that emphasizing positive self-esteem strengthens Christian values. I make this assertion because when I show caregivers how to assess self-esteem in a valid and reliable fashion, interpret results of assessments and identify those participants who require special assistance, I assist them in saving human lives; when I show caregivers how to develop and implement effective self-esteem enhancement programs, I help them save human lives; when I teach parents strategies that enhance the self-esteem of their children, I assist them in promoting the development of their offspring.

I consider the behaviors listed above to be consistent with Christian values, as I understand them.

THE IMPORTANCE OF SELF-ESTEEM

Dorothy Briggs, a major contributor in the field, summarizes her views regarding the importance of self-esteem in the following fashion:

"A person's judgment of self, influences the kind of friends he chooses, how he gets along with others, the kind of person he marries, and how productive he will be. It affects his creativity, integrity, stability, and even whether he will be a leader or a follower. His feeling of self worth forms the core of his personality and determines the use he makes of his aptitudes and abilities. His attitude toward himself has a direct bearing on how he lives all parts of his life. In fact, self-esteem is the main spring that slates each of us for success or failure as a human being..."

Another major contributor Nathaniel Branden expresses his views regarding the importance of Self-Esteem in the following fashion:

"...Apart from problems that are biological in origin, I cannot think of a single psychological difficulty... that is not traceable to poor self-esteem. Of all the judgments we pass, none is as important as the one we pass on ourselves. Positive self-esteem is a cardinal requirement of a fulfilling life..."

I, *(Battle, 1992, p.22; 1993, p.19)* propose that self-esteem affects one's:

- Accomplishments

- Interactions with others

- Achievement patterns

- Levels of mental health

- State of well being

Nathaniel Branden, *(1960)* offers the following regarding the need of Self-Esteem.

There is no value judgment more important to man; no factor more decisive in his psychological development and motivation than the estimate he possesses of himself. This estimate is ordinarily experienced by him, not in the form of a conscious, verbalized judgment, but in terms of a feeling; a feeling that can be hard to isolate and identify because he experiences it constantly; it is part of every other feeling; it is involved in his every emotional response. Man's view of himself is necessarily implicit in all value responses. Any judgment entailing the issue, "Is this for me or against me?" entails a view of the "me" involved. His self-evaluation is an omnipotent factor in man's psychology. The nature of his self-evaluation has profound effects on an individual's thinking processes, emotions, desires, values and goals. It is the single most significant key to his behavior. To understand an individual psychologically, one must understand the nature and degree of his self-esteem and the standards by which he judges himself *(pp. 109-110).*

In the following, I share my views regarding the importance of Children and the need to nourish their self-esteem.

THE SELF-ESTEEM POEM

*Children may be happy or
they may be sad
Children may misbehave,
but they are never bad
Children require love and
protection
Given freely without conditions
and rejection
Children's needs are deep and long
When loved unconditionally they
will grow up to be strong
Children need encouragement
and opportunities to be heard and seen
in order to develop positive
self-esteem
Children strive for excitement and thrill
with proper love and respect their
dreams will be fulfilled.*

James Battle

LOW SELF-ESTEEM

In his list of characteristics associated with individuals experiencing low self-esteem, Coopersmith (1967) offered the following:

1. Individuals with low self-esteem tend to withdraw from others and experience consistent feelings of distress.

2. People with low self-esteem tend to be more intropunitive and passive in adapting to environmental demands and pressures than

individuals who possess high self-esteem.

3. Low self-esteem tends to be equated with inferiority, timidity, self-hatred, lack of personal acceptance, and submissiveness.

4. People low in self-esteem tend to exhibit higher levels of anxiety and are more likely to exhibit more frequent psychosomatic symptoms and feelings of depression than individuals with high self-esteem.

5. People with low self-esteem tend to be isolates who seldom select one another. These individuals tend to feel that they have greater difficulties forming friendships than do others. There does not appear to be any relationship however, between self-esteem and group membership. Persons of all levels of confidence and assurance are equally likely to join social groups, but the roles they play are different.

6. Low self-esteem individuals tend not to resist social pressures.

7. Individuals with low self-esteem are more likely to remain quiet if they feel dissent will evoke personal attack. They are often unwilling to express controversal opinions, even when they know they are correct; and they tend to have strong, defensive reactions to criticism.

8. Low self-esteem individuals tend to be "invisible" members of a group; they rarely serve as leaders.

9. Low self-esteem individuals tend to lack confidence to respect the critical appraisal of others, and remain defeated and exposed in their real or imagined deficiencies.

10. Individuals with low self-esteem tend to be self-conscious of their inadequacies – whether real or imagined.

11. Low self-esteem-individuals, when distracted by personal concerns, will likely turn inward and dwell upon themselves unlike those with high self-esteem.

In addition to Coopersmith's list, I believe that the following are additional characteristics of individuals who possess low self-esteem (*1982, pp. 41-43*):

1. Low self-esteem individuals tend to be low in initiative and basically non-assertive in their interactions with others.

2. Low self-esteem individuals tend to be more anxious than individuals who possess high self-esteem. These individuals tend to worry and to be pessimistic in their views concerning the future.

3. Low self-esteem individuals tend to be more prone to employing the defenses of projection and repression than individuals who esteem themselves highly.

4. Low self-esteem individuals tend to be more susceptible to developing obsessive-compulsive reactions than people who esteem themselves highly.

5. Low self-esteem individuals tend to be more timid, shy, and predisposed to withdrawal than individuals who esteem themselves highly.

6. Low self-esteem people tend to be indecisive and usually vacillate when confronted with obstacles.

7. Low self-esteem individuals are more prone to emitting self-defeating responses and developing

self-punishing modes of behavior than individuals who esteem themselves highly.

8. Low self-esteem individuals tend to conform more readily to social pressure and exhibit a greater degree of dependence than individuals who esteem themselves highly.

PSEUDO-SELF-ESTEEM

Nathaniel Branden (1969) and J. Battle (1982, 1987) propose that self-esteem is a fundamental need of humans at all developmental levels. Self-esteem is a powerful force which exerts a strong effect on all humans. Support for this position is provided by Branden (1969), who states that self-esteem is a need that cannot be avoided; and that those who fail to achieve self-esteem, or who fail to a significant degree in their search for self-esteem, strive to fake it. Because they fail to ascertain self-esteem, they attempt to hide behind a facade and display pseudo self-esteem. Pseudo or inauthentic self-esteem, according to Branden, is an irrational pretense of self-value. It is a non-rational self-protective device designed to reduce anxiety and enhance a sense of security. It (inauthentic self-esteem), is maintained by the use of defense mechanisms, (e.g. rationalization or false but acceptable excuses created for one's unacceptable behavior; denial or refusal to admit realities; projection or attributing one's own behavior or characteristics to others). Authentic self-esteem on the other hand, is maintained or enhanced by actions that are in concert with the individual's moral code. The authentic individual is motivated by reality and emits behaviors that are consistent with his standards. He is confident in himself and is motivated by love of self, whereas the inauthentic individual is defensive and motivated by fear that he is not worthy. Branden (*1969*) lists the following categories of defenses which he feels inauthentic individuals generally employ:

The man who is obsessed with being popular, who feels driven to win the approval of every person he meets, who clings to the image of himself as "likeable," who in effect, regards his appealing personality as his means of survival and the proof of his personal worth.

The woman who has no sense of personal identity and who seeks to lose her inner emptiness in the role of a sacrificial martyr for her children, demanding in exchange "only" that her children adore her, that their adoration fill the vacuum of the ego she does not possess.

The man who never forms independent judgments about anything, but who seeks to compensate by making himself authoritatively knowledgeable concerning other men's opinions about everything.

The man who works at being aggressively "masculine," whose other concerns are entirely subordinated to his role as woman-chaser, and who derives less pleasure from the act of sex than from the act of reporting his adventures to the men in the locker room.

The woman whose chief standard of self-appraisal is the "prestige" of her husband, and whose pseudo-self-esteem rises or falls according to the number of men who court her husband's favor.

The man who feels guilt over having inherited a fortune, who has no idea of what to do with it, and proceeds frantically to give it away, clinging to the "ideal" of altruism and to the vision of himself as a humanitarian, keeping his pseudo-self-esteem afloat by the belief that charity is a moral substitute for competence and courage.

The man who has always been afraid of life and who tells himself that the reason he is superior is "sensitivity," who chooses his clothes, his furniture, his books, and his bodily posture by the standard of what will make him appear idealistic (*p.151*).

HEALTHY SELF-ESTEEM

I, (*Battle, 2007*) propose that individuals at all levels of development who possess healthy self-esteem (high to very high levels of self-esteem as measured by The Culture-Free Self-Esteem Inventories):

- Experience success in areas that are important to them
- Realize that they are worthy whether others recognize this or not
- Realize that they do not have to be perfect to be worthwhile
- Possess levels of autonomy that enable them to think for themselves and do what they consider to be best
- Possess the courage they need to do what they consider to be appropriate
- Respect themselves and others

Individuals with healthy self-esteem do not:

- Worry excessively about what they think others think
- Experience excessive symptoms of anxiety
- Experience excessive symptoms of depression
- Experience symptoms of suicidal ideation

In the following statement, I share my view regarding my self-esteem.

MY SELF-ESTEEM

My Self-Esteem is not:

Contingent on

What

Others Think

What

Others Say

What

Others Do

Rather it is a:

Product of my

Subjective perception

Source: Battle, 2007

I encourage you to use your authentic self-esteem and information in this section to assist you in your efforts to do God's will.

MISSION AND SERVICE

At our facility we have provided a wide variety of free services for participants including:

- Purchased and donated clothing
- Psychotherapy
- Movie passes

The other services that we have provided include:

- Employment training
- Life skills and employability skills training
- Drinks and snacks

- A complimentary copy of the book entitled "9 to 19: Crucial Years For Self-Esteem In Children And Youth"

- A complimentary copy of an audiocassette tape entitled "Effective Parenting Tips That Build Self-Esteem"

- A complimentary copy of an audiocassette entitled "Strategies That You Can Use To Enhance Your Own Self-Esteem"

- A complimentary copy of a book entitled "Strategies That You Can Use To Enhance Your Own Self-Esteem And Well Being"

- Academic Upgrading

- An opportunity to receive General Educational Development (G.E.D.) training and tutoring

- Five (5) dollars to open his or her own personal bank savings account

- Registration fees for enrolment in advanced educational programs

- Tickets to professional football games

- Bus passes and tickets

- Opportunity to be treated by our physician partner without the need for scheduled appointments

- Opportunity to receive legal representation from our lawyer partner

I believe that God set me aside at birth and called me to serve. However, I didn't realize this until I was in my forties when I drove a teenager named Young Chief home. When I stopped in front of her apartment, she said, you are my angel sent by God to serve me. If you, Dr. Battle, did not come into my life, I would not be alive.

The following are some unsolicited comments provided by individuals that my wife and I had the privilege of serving:

Report 1: Personal Comments

To Dr. Battle,

Thank you very much for giving me the greatest gift I have ever gotten. That gift is the support and courage that you have given. If it weren't for you, I would not have the strength to get out of bed in the morning or carry on with my day. I never would have carried on with my education or get off Social Services, I am doing both in less than two months. You are an incredible man with amazing talent. For all that you have done, I thank you!

All my love and respect,

Report 2: Personal Comments

Dear Dr. Battle,

I hope you are well and doing fine, I'm writing to thank you for all the help you've given me over the years. I believe. I would not be here if it hadn't been for your help. My life was a mess. I hid my drinking problem from you so well, I didn't even know I had a problem myself, thankfully my life came to a crash on July 10, 1993. I was insane that night. Today I am sober and have turned my life around one-hundred and eighty degrees.

G.S. 1999

Report 3: Personal Comments

Dear Dr. Battle,

I want to say thank you very much for giving and providing me with such powerful, strong, positive advice and words of wisdom during our talks that we have had together which brings my self-esteem and confidence in myself increasing immensely everyday of my life.

You are a wonderful man to me who has the utmost care and respect for me in my special characteristics and qualities that are a part of my upbringing in life.

Yours truly,

Report 4: Personal Comments

Dear Dr. Battle,

As a former student who walked in with very little self-esteem and less thought as to what I was going to do with my life, I thought it was about time that I sent a note to say thank you. It has been many years and I have had time to slow my life to take the time to think how I have gotten here. It was not until recently that I realized that yes I did get something out of your training course. (Self-confidence) to pick up each time I fell.

I remember you saying that even if one could be saved then it is worth all the work. If it was not for the kick in the ass you gave me when I needed it, I would not have gone back to Alberta Vocational College and I would not have had the courage to fall and get back up. I am an Allocation Analyst with one of the largest and most complicated Natural Gas Companies in North America (Westcoast Field Services). It did not start out that way of course there was 2 years of school pain Staten and 1 ½ years of bad paying secretarial jobs, with barely enough to make it by.

Report 5: Personal Comments

Dear Dr. Battle,

I have been meaning to write you a letter for a long time regarding how grateful and happy I am that I had the opportunity to be in your job training program in 1995. I really believe I am happy and successful because of this program.

Before I came to the program I was having a hard time getting a job and was told there was no point going back to school because it costs money and I wasn't very good at. I had low self-esteem and my doctor wanted to put me on an antidepressant.

Through your self-esteem counselling I learned how to accept my self and never to make excuses or pity myself so that I couldn't accomplish something. I always remember Dr. Battle saying, "the past is the past now let's focus on the future." I also know if I am starting to feel down that I look at where that negativity is coming from and usually have to hold back from the "poisonous people." Since the program I feel I am a positive person and I have not needed an antidepressant for depression.

The program also taught me to love education and to be a life long learner. In the program I did some upgrading and since then I have become a certified Ophthalmic assistant, taken psychology 104 and 105 and a Doula training course (birth assistant). This also rubbed off on my husband who went back to school and graduated with a diploma in Telecommunications.

Since the program I have worked for 5 years as an Ophthalmic assistant, bought a house, had a baby and now starting my own business as a pre and post birth assistant.

I don't know any other program to have such a lasting effect. I am truly grateful that the government sponsored this program and that you were running it because you both are very good at what you do and you know to guide those of us that needed to be guided.

Thank you so much, D.H.

Report 6: Personal Comments

Dear Dr. & Mrs. James Battle,

I would like to express my appreciation for the Modern Office Specialist program headed by you in July 1997. I feel the training program has provided me with above average skills needed in an office environment.

I would like to keep you up to date on my progress since graduating from your program in December 1997. I worked as a Junior Accountant at Diamondwest Sales Inc. from December 1997 until August 1998. I worked beneath the Controller who was very pleased with my skills and knowledge of the position. I left Diamondwest Sales Inc. in August 1998 and accepted a position at Anderson Career Training Institute as an office manager.

I have now been at Anderson for over a year. My co-workers are great and the pay is wonderful. I would like you to know I have used the program to my full advantage and I feel the training has been beneficial. I feel I am very lucky to have been given the opportunity to expand on my skills and appreciate the position I am now holding.

I have also come to the conclusion that I enjoy working with finances, and have decided to pursue my education further. I am currently in my first year of the Bachelor of Commerce program at Athabasca University.

I am very happy with the direction my life has taken. Thank you very much for having me in your program.

Sincerely

Report 7: Personal Comments

Dear Dr. & Mrs. James Battle,

When this program started, I was taught about Self Esteem. Self Esteem has increased my ability to look at life in a new perspective. My family, my education, and myself has improved steady since the information of self-esteem has been brought to my attention by Dr. James Battle.

For myself, self-esteem gave me insight to which I am, to what I've become, and how to improve myself. I've learned that failure is just a set back and a task can be tackled not without a fight. I've also learned to believe in myself, that I'm worthwhile, no matter what demeaning attempts others may say. Self esteem brought improvement in my life.

Self-esteem has improved my family as well. My husband has noticed a change in me, and this scared him. For my husband has always seen me depressed, and just like that, my negative vibes turned into positive energy. I've talked to my husband about my new perspective on life and he wanted to do the same. I guess this positive energy has worn off on him. Also with my children I've used reflective listening. Children need to be heard and the conversations I have with my children are more meaningful. Self-esteem has made an improvement in my family.

Self-esteem has opened my eyes in a different positive view.

I thank Dr. James Battle, he has given me more than a helping hand. He has passed his knowledge down to me and I truly thank him.

Report 8: Personal Comments

Dear Dr. & Mrs. James Battle,

It has now been just over a year since I finished your course and started working at Custom Lighting. I thought that now would be a good time to thank you for reaching out to me at a time when it seemed no one would.

I will always appreciate everything that you helped me accomplish.

Thank you.

Report 9: Personal Comments

Dr. Battle and Dorothy,

I'm going to describe what Dr. Battle's program did for me. When I entered the program, I felt like a lost puppy. I had no sense of direction. I didn't have a clue on what life had to offer, and most importantly, I had very poor self-esteem. I felt the world was against me, since nothing went right for me. I felt like I would never amount to anything, and I never gave myself credit for anything I did. I felt like a nobody, and that life was nothing but a non-ending vicious circle.

Even with the doubts I had in my mind, I took a chance for the first time in ... well, I couldn't remember how long. I thought, "Well, what IF what this man tells me could be true? I could be passing up a fantastic opportunity". And not very many had come my way in quite a while. So I stuck around, not really being aware that what Dr. Battle was teaching me was actually sinking in. I came to actually like myself, and like others around me, I loved being around others, who were here for the same reasons I was, and it was amazing how I could relate to them. I felt life had treated me so unfair, until I heard other similar (if not worse) horror stories on life.

Then I realized that life isn't fair, but you have to make the most of it. The past is the past, and that's where it belongs. You can't change the past, but you sure can improve the future.

So what could the objectives be behind the program? Well, I will always praise Dr. Battle and his Associates, since it gave me my life back. There had been so much that I had lost, and through this program, I found it all again. I now feel like a somebody (even an important one), and I feel alive. I regained my self-confidence, my self-worth, and a good self-image. I feel refreshed, and if anyone would have asked me a year ago what I hoped to be doing a year from now, I would've probably said, "I don't care." But I don't know that person anymore, and I don't want to. I now have hopes and dreams, and a brand new life.

I learned that if you want something in life, it never gets handed to you. You have to work at what you want, and getting it all depends on what you put into it. I now have a job, a better education, and I learned to do some soul-searching. My attitude has changed so much, and my outlook on life is a positive one.

I will always thank you, Dr. Battle and Dorothy, for popping into my life. You had so much to offer, and this might be sort of a selfish thing to say, but I have taken full advantage of what you had to teach me. Thank you for having confidence in me when no one else did... not even me.

Report 10: Personal Comments

It's been eight years since I've contacted you, Dr. Battle, and I hope you remember me as you did 5 years ago when I last needed your help. This is...writing to you, and actually, I didn't get to see or thank you for your help in 1998 when I was in a crisis...I had the chance to visit a bit with Dorothy (and Maria) in your office. I was in your course back in 1991, and in your video of comprehensive strategies (still have my copy!) and your words came to me... "Once you are in Dr. Battle's family, you're there for life" I am still in B.C. as I write you, and was planning a visit to Edmonton before Nov 26th for the Baroque Masterworks Exhibit at the Alberta Art Gallery) and your name came to me as I was cooking supper the other night, and I know that God lead me to research you and know that I must see you when I come since I no longer think I'm coming for a visit, I feel as though my guides have been nudging me for years, but eventually they turn into kicks and I now have the faith, courage and strength to finally face all my demons that have trapped me for so many years tucked up safe in the mountains. I have to change my family dynamics...and it does not come without pain to leave my children for the moment where they are safe and secure (...is now 18 yrs old, ...is 10 yrs old), but I, and they, now know I must get out of this environment for my own happiness. This is the hardest thing I've had to do...I'm at a point where faith is all I have. But I do know your name came to me for a reason. You have seen me through a couple crises, and I know I can turn to you for support and resources like no one I know. I have a place to stay rent free with a friend that lives a "clean" life...who will be of much support so I can build myself a life, so that I can accommodate my children in the future. This is very important to me, since drugs (marijuana) has been one factor in this lifestyle that I have battled repeatedly over the years. I will need counselling Dr. Battle, since I've been at this crossroads many times over the last 12 years, but this time there is no turning back. I have already written a book, but I will leave the rest for when I can see you even briefly. I thought I would give you a head's up before I showed up one day soon. I so look forward to seeing you and Dorothy again. You taught me how to shine, and shine again I will, letting go and letting God. I thank the angels for speaking your name in my ear... and thank my gift of intuition for listening, already knowing it will lead me to where I need to be.

My wife Dorothy and I tell all of our students that when they graduate from our program they become members of the Battle family and that we will always make ourselves available to serve them after program completion. On September 15, 2007, a graduate of our employment program was blessed with a lottery win of $8.8 million dollars. In a news paper article, the twenty-nine year old was quoted as saying... They said I couldn't walk and I refused to believe that. I walked out of there (hospital) six months later...

The statement listed above is consistent with knowledge incorporated in the strategy entitled "positive thinking and perseverance promotes success" that we teach our students and clients. Also, it is in concert with my poem entitled "Show Them" (see page 88).

The individual's intentions to use the lottery win to establish an educational trust fund for fifteen nieces and nephews and two foster siblings is in concert with our teachings regarding mission and commitment.

Instruction derived from Christian tenets effects beliefs, perception and behavior. The knowledge provided in this chapter which addresses an effective therapeutic approach, the need of self-esteem and the importance of mission and service can be used to assist individuals in obtaining personal goals and achieving desired results.

SUMMARY

- Beliefs are powerful.

- Practice makes improvement.

- Rational Eclectic Therapy is an effective psychotherapeutic approach.

- The Ten Commandments provides instructions for supporters of the Christian faith.

- The Apostle's Creed is a core statement of belief for supporters of the Christian faith.

- The Lord's Prayer is an essential element of the Christian faith.

- Love jealousy is compelled by caring.

- Hate jealousy is compelled by the desire to hurt or injury.

- Self-esteem is a subjective perception that individuals possess regarding their own worth.

- Perception is the major force compelling behavior.

- Emphasing self-esteem does not weaken Christian values

- Self-esteem is an important human need.

- Self-esteem is a fundamental need which affects the lives of individuals at all stages of development.

- Self-esteem is the most important variable that influences success.

- Some individuals experience pseudo or inauthentic self-esteem.

- Mission and service are important elements of the Christian faith.

PART III

Faith and Mission

CHAPTER 3

GOD'S COMMANDS AND ENVIRONMENTAL DEMANDS

In THIS CHAPTER, WE DESCRIBE STRATEGIES that individuals can use in their efforts to do God's will. Christians, like other individuals function best when they have effective knowledge that they can use to do God's work while dealing with environmental demands. The Cognitive (Thinking) Strategies that I have found to be beneficial to me during my efforts to accomplish both of these tasks are:

The A-B-C Paradigm

The Ten Step Count Down

Reflective Listening

Positive Actions Strategies

Mutual Respect

Encouragement

THE A-B-C PARADIGM

The A-B-C Paradigm is a cognitive strategy that Battle (*1990, 1992, 1993, 1994, 1997*) have found to be effective in assisting in controlling feelings, solving problems and emitting behavior that is self-enhancing rather than self-defeating. This strategy is effective because thought or cognition, how you feel and subsequently behave is basically determined by how you think. When using the A-B-C Paradigm it is important for you to realize that:

A is: What others say or do

What happens in the external environment

B is: How you feel, which is determined by how you think and what you tell yourself about what others say or do at point A

C is: What you do or say

It is important for you to realize that what others say or do at point A does not determine how you feel. Rather, it is what you tell yourself (internalized self-verbalizations or thoughts that typically operate at an unconscious level) that determines how you feel. Therefore, if a person calls you a "bad" name, and you become angry, it is not the name calling that makes you angry. Rather, it is what you tell yourself at point B about the name calling that makes you angry; chances are if a very young child called you the same name that the older youth or adult called you, you wouldn't become angry.

A-B-C PARADIGM: A LIFE SAVING MODEL

The following incidents cited by Battle (2001) in his book entitled "Dealing With Anger: Strategies That Work", would have yielded different results if those involved employed the A-B-C Paradigm.

I: Youth kills youth on New Years Eve while attending a party celebrating his 18th birthday.

Result: Eighteen year old stabs and kills 17 year old

*Victim stabbed several times with a kitchen knife

II: Youth killed while walking home after celebrating her eighteenth birthday.

Result: Eighteen year old shot and killed after confrontation at a nightclub

III: Youth killed at party

Result: Youth killed while hosting a party at his

parents home

IV: Seventeen year old killed while attending birthday celebration.

Result: Youth stabbed to death at a private party in a community hall

V: Twenty year old killed while celebrating fatherhood

Result: Father to be, stabbed to death while partying

VI: Road Rage Hits Respectable Woman

Result: Mother of one child kills enraged mother of three children

*Mother opened the glove compartment of her car, took out her revolver and killed the victim when she shot her in the face.

VII: Men plead guilty to manslaughter in road rage case

Result: Men kill victim when they hit him on the head with a baseball bat.

THE A-B-C PARADIGM: AN EFFECTIVE TOOL

I, Battle (2006) author of the book entitled "Dealing With Anger: Strategies That Work", propose that:

If incidents are not premeditated the number of

- Violent acts would be
- Reduced significantly

If

- Participating individuals employed the
- A-B-C Paradigm prior to the

- Commencement of the

- Display of behavior

I encourage individuals to employ the knowledge incorporated in the following to assist themselves in their efforts to achieve desired results:

Using The A-B-C Paradigm to Deal With Issues:

I. SEX

- Should I participate in sexual intercourse?

- Should I require my partner to use a condom?

- Should I encourage my partner to use birth control methods?

(e.g. birth control pills; diaphragms)

II. ALCOHOL ABUSE

- Should I ingest alcohol?

- When drinking, should I limit the amount of alcohol I intake?

- Should I use alcohol when I have problems?

- Should I associate with individuals who are addicted to alcohol?

- Should I ride in vehicles driven by individuals who have been drinking alcohol?

III. ILLEGAL DRUG ABUSE

- Should I ingest illegal drugs?

- Should I associate with individuals who are addicted to illegal drugs?

- Should I attend social gatherings where illegal drugs are being used?

IV. ACADEMIC ACHIEVEMENT

- Should I attend classes on a regular basis?

- Should I complete classroom and homework assignments?

- Should I cooperate with teachers and other authority figures?

- Should I stay in school and complete my program?

V. BEHAVIORAL MANAGEMENT

- Should I obey rules and regulations established by:

1. Parents

2. Teachers

3. Employers

4. Legal authorities, church leaders

- Should I learn strategies that will assist in managing behavior more appropriately to reduce the probability of becoming a participant in hostile or violent confrontations?

VI. EMPLOYMENT

- Should I learn strategies that will assist me in performing more efficiently at work?

- Should I develop strategies that will assist me in avoiding absenteeism and tardiness at work?

- Should I improve my ability to interact effectively with co-workers?

- Should I improve my ability to interact effectively with employers?

VII. SEXUALLY TRANSMITTED DISEASES

• Should I increase my knowledge of sexually transmitted diseases?

• Should I require my partner to undergo examinations for sexually transmitted diseases prior to making a decision regarding sexual intercourse?

VIII. DOING GOD'S WILL

• Should I join a Christian church?

• Should I attend worship services on a regular basis?

• Should I volunteer to serve the poor?

• Should I commit myself to extending God's Kingdom?

• Should I commit myself to promoting the Christian faith?

In each of the situations listed above you can make decisions at B (by using internalized self-verbalizations) that will increase the probability of you behaving in ways that increase the probability of you achieving desired results.

A-B-C Paradigm: An Illustration

A

What others say or do

B

How you feel about what others say or do

C

What you say or do

Both Christians and non-Christians can use the above illustration to help them think about an action and its consequences before emitting the behavior.

Those employing this strategy learn to realize how they feel is not determined by what others do at A, but rather is due to what they tell themselves at point B. Also, employing the A-B-C Paradigm enables the individual to think about the probable consequences of an action before emitting the behavior. Thus, the Christian can employ this strategy to assist him or her in efforts to emit behavior that is in concert with Christian beliefs and God's commandments. I realize that how I feel and what I do is determined by what I tell myself at point B. Therefore, I don't make myself upset at point B and let God work within me and because of this I typically emit behavior at C that is self-enhancing rather than self-defeating.

THE TEN-STEP COUNTDOWN PROCEDURE

The Ten-Step Countdown is a cognitive procedure that can be used to control impulsivity while interacting with others, which will in turn assist you in dealing effectively with the negative behavior of others and increase the probability of you achieving success in spite of the actions of others.

When using the Ten-Step Countdown Procedure, count down from ten to one (e.g. 10, 9, 8, 7, 6, 5, 4, 3, 2, 1) at a rate of about one digit per second before responding overtly to an environmental stimulus. For example, when responding to "name calling" or attempts at "put-downs", count backwards slowly from ten to one before reacting overtly to the "name calling" or attempts at "put-downs". By doing this, it increases the probability that you will emit behavior that results in positive consequences. Similarly, if a child or adult is called a "bad" name his initial impulse may be to respond in a similar fashion and call the initiator a bad name or fight. However, if the child or adult who is the victim of "name-calling" employs the Ten-Step Countdown Procedure immediately prior to responding overtly, the employment of this strategy will increase the probability of him or her emitting behavior that is self-enhancing rather than self-defeating.

The Ten-Step Countdown Procedure can be used effectively in conjunction with the A-B-C Paradigm described earlier in this section. For instance, you may use the A-B-C Paradigm initially in your attempts to control arousal and immediately afterwards follow up with the Ten-Step Countdown in your attempts to control impulsivity and emit behavior that is self-enhancing.

The Ten Step Countdown Procedure is an effective tool for you to use in your efforts to do God's Will and deal with environmental demands.

REFLECTIVE LISTENING

Reflective Listening is a strategy that you can use to solve problems. Being able to achieve resolutions to problems that we are confronted with generally exerts a positive effect on relationships.

Reflective Listening is a cognitive procedure in which a significant other communicates to a person that he or she recognizes the feelings that are associated with what he is saying. For example, your friend may say, "I hate my boss; he is unfair." To reflect your friend's feelings you may say, "It appears that you are angry and disappointed at how things are going to work."

Use the strategy of Reflective Listening to assist others and yourself in achieving resolutions to problems. When assisting others:

First, reflect the person's feelings so that he or she feels understood.

Then, help the person clarify the problem precisely.

And third, help the person solve the problem he or she is confronted with by:

A. Exploring alternatives

B. Assessing the consequences of alternatives, and

C. Choosing modes of behavior that are self-enhancing rather than self-defeating.

Let's use the case of Mary to illustrate how the three basic steps involved in the Reflective Listening process can be used to help others solve problems.

Mary, a 28-year-old employee, very emotionally says to her friend, "I hate my job, the work is boring."

STEP 1 REFLECTION: To reflect Mary's feelings, her friend may say "It seems like you are disappointed with how things are going at work."

STEP 2 CLARIFICATION: Mary may say, "Well, it's not work that is the problem. It's my co-workers Tom and Bob who bug me at work."

STEP 3 RESOLUTION: Mary's friend may say,

"What do you think you can do to stop Tom and Bob from bugging you at work?"

Mary can then explore alternatives. For example "I can ask my boss to stop them from bugging me." or "I can confront Tom and Bob and tell them to stop bugging me." or "I can use rational thought and stop making myself upset because of their behavior."

At this point, Mary's friend may say, "What do you feel would happen if you asked your boss to stop them from bugging you?" By asking this she is assessing the consequences of alternatives.

Mary may say, "My boss would probably think that I can't handle my own problems."

Then Mary's friend may say, "What do you think would happen if you confronted Tom and Bob and told them to stop bugging you?"

Mary may say, "They would probably become defensive and bug me even more."

Going on, Mary's friend may say, "What do you think would happen if you used rational thought?"

Mary may then say, "If I don't make myself upset their behavior would not bug me."

To help Mary choose modes of behavior that are self - enhancing rather than self-defeating, Mary's friend might then say, "What do you feel is best?" or "What choice will work best for you?"

Mary would probably say, "To use rational thought and stop making myself upset because of their behavior."

Use the same procedure delineated above when you are confronted with problems. First, clarify the problem precisely; then:

A. Explore alternatives

B. Assess the consequences of alternatives

C. Choose modes of behavior that are self-enhancing.

You can use the Reflective Listening Cognitive Strategy to achieve resolution to both routine and complicated problems and assist you in your efforts to do God's will and deal with environmental demands. When confronted with problems I use Reflective Listening and integrate it with my belief and faith in God and his Son Jesus Christ.

POSITIVE ACTION STRATEGIES

Use the following Positive Action Strategies in your efforts to maintain and strengthen your Christian faith, do God's will and deal with environmental demands.

When using these positive action strategies:

- Don't utilize your energy complaining about negative actions directed towards you by others; instead use your energy to determine what you will do about what others did to you and DO IT.

- View setbacks as learning experiences and use the knowledge derived from them to assist you in obtaining success.

- Write specific goals and put into action strategies that will enable you to achieve them.

- Realize that you are worthy whether others recognize this basic fact or not and use your talents effectively.

- Realize that you don't have to be perfect to be worthwhile; that perfection in personality does not exist; recognize your strengths and limitations and strive to be the best that you can be.

- Realize that your future is not necessarily dependent on your past; the experiences of your past do not necessarily dictate what will happen to you in the present or future.

- Do not utilize a significant amount of your energy worrying about things you cannot control.

MUTUAL RESPECT

In your efforts to do God's will and deal with environmental demands provide others mutual respect.

Mutual Respect is a cognitive procedure in which significant others communicate to an individual that he or she is respected as a unique person possessing the same basic rights and responsibilities as others of similar age, and status.

Complete the following inventory to determine the level of mutual respect you provide others while interacting with them.

THE MUTUAL RESPECT INVENTORY FOR ADULTS, FORM A

James Battle, Ph.D.

Directions: Please mark each question in the following way. For each of the questions there are five options for response: always, usually, sometimes, seldom, never. Put a check mark on the option that most closely describes what you do. Please check only one option for each of the 10 questions. This is not a test, and there are no "right" or "wrong" answers.

1. Do you let others know that you feel that they are just as good as you are?

☐ always ☐ usually ☐ sometimes ☐ seldom ☐ never

2. Do you provide others mutual respect when interacting with them?

☐ always ☐ usually ☐ sometimes ☐ seldom ☐ never

3. Do you communicate to others that your caring for them is unconditional?

☐ always ☐ usually ☐ sometimes ☐ seldom ☐ never

4. Do you interact with others in a non-judgmental fashion?

☐ always ☐ usually ☐ sometimes ☐ seldom ☐ never

5. Do you respect the point- of -view of others even if it is different from yours?

☐ always ☐ usually ☐ sometimes ☐ seldom ☐ never

6. Do you minimize the importance of the mistakes that others make?

☐ always ☐ usually ☐ sometimes ☐ seldom ☐ never

7. Do you let others know that you appreciate their contributions?

☐ always ☐ usually ☐ sometimes ☐ seldom ☐ never

8. Do you avoid criticizing others when they make mistakes?

☐ always ☐ usually ☐ sometimes ☐ seldom ☐ never

9. Do you emphasize the positive aspects of the behavior of others?

☐ always ☐ usually ☐ sometimes ☐ seldom ☐ never

10. Do you consider the effects that your actions can have on the self-esteem of others when interacting with them?

    ☐ always ☐ usually ☐ sometimes ☐ seldom ☐ never

Score

Score The Mutual Respect Inventory in the following fashion.

Always yields a score of 5 for each of the ten items; the value for Usually is 4; whereas Sometimes earns a score of 3; Seldom yields a score of 2; and Never yields a score of 1.

The highest possible score you can earn on The Mutual Respect Inventory is 50 whereas the lowest possible score is 10. Use the Classification of scores listed in table 3.1 to rate the level of mutual respect you provide others.

Table 3.1 Classification of Scores For The Mutual Respect Inventory For Adults, Form A	
Score	**Classification**
42 +	Very High
39 – 41	High
28 – 38	Intermediate
23 – 27	Low
22 -	Very Low

Interpretation

Interpretation

If you earned a score of 42 or above, your level of mutual respect is very high; a score ranging between 39 to 41 indicates that your level of mutual respect is high; whereas those scores between 28 and 38 indicate that you tend to provide an intermediate or average level of mutual respect to others, while a score of 27 or below indicates that you tend to provide to others low to very low levels of mutual respect when interacting with them.

The following statement supports the position that proposes that humans need to respect one another.

An Essential Christian Commandment: Christ Said

- A new commandment I give you that

- You love one another; thus he instructed Christians not to

- Envy their neighbors and to

- Treat them the way that we want them to treat us

ENCOURAGEMENT

The important role that encouragement plays in the lives of humans is expressed in 1 Thessalonians 5:11 as follows:

> "...Therefore, keep comforting one another and building one another up, just as you are in fact doing..."

In your efforts to do God's will and deal with environmental demands, provide those with whom you select to interact as colleagues and friends with encouragement. Encouragement is a cognitive procedure in which a significant other emphasizes the positive aspects of an individual's behavior rather than the negative aspects. That is, the person providing the encouragement minimizes the importance of an individual's mistakes while recognizing his or her assets and strengths.

Encouragement is important because if you encourage others they will return the same, and assist you in your efforts to achieve desired results. Complete the following inventory to determine the level of encouragement you provide to others while interacting with them.

THE ENCOURAGEMENT INVENTORY FOR ADULTS, FORM A

James Battle, Ph.D.

Directions: Please mark each question in the following way. For each of the questions there are five options for response: "always"," usually", "sometimes", "seldom", and "never". Put a check mark (√) on the option that most closely describes what you do. Please check only one option for each of the 10 questions. This is not a test, and there are no "right", or "wrong" answers.

1. Do you encourage others to strive to succeed?

☐ always ☐ usually ☐ sometimes ☐ seldom ☐ never

2. Do you provide others mutual respect while interacting with them?

☐ always ☐ usually ☐ sometimes ☐ seldom ☐ never

3. Do you consider the effects that your actions can have on the self-esteem of others when interacting with them?

☐ always ☐ usually ☐ sometimes ☐ seldom ☐ never

4. Do you provide others recognition for their effort and achievement?

☐ always ☐ usually ☐ sometimes ☐ seldom ☐ never

5. Do you emphasize the positive aspects of the behavior of others?

□ always □ usually □ sometimes □ seldom □ never

6. Do you minimize the importance of the mistakes that others make?

□ always □ usually □ sometimes □ seldom □ never

7. Do you tell others that you appreciate their contributions?

□ always □ usually □ sometimes □ seldom □ never

8. Do you co-operate with others and provide them support when they desire it?

□ always □ usually □ sometimes □ seldom □ never

9. Do you interact with others in a non-judgemental fashion?

□ always □ usually □ sometimes □ seldom □ never

10. Do you communicate to others that your caring for them is unconditional?

□ always □ usually □ sometimes □ seldom □ never

Score

Score The Encouragement Inventory in the following fashion.

Always yields a score of 5 for each of the ten items: the value for Usually is 4; whereas Sometimes earns a score of 3; Seldom yields a score of 2; while Never yields a score of 1.

The highest possible score you can earn on The Encouragement Inventory is 50, whereas the lowest possible score is 10. Use the Classification of scores listed in the Table 3:2 to rate the level of encouragement you provide to others.

Table 3:2 Classification of Scores For The Encouragement Inventory For Adults, Form A	
Score	Classification
45 + ...Very High	
40 - 44 ....High	
28 - 39 ....Intermediate	
23 - 27 ....Low	
22 - ....Very Low	

Source: Battle, J. 1995. The Encouragement Inventory. Edmonton, AB., James Battle and Associates Ltd.

Interpretation

If you earned a score of 45 or above, your level of encouragement is very high; a score ranging between 40 to 44 indicates that your value is high; whereas those between 28 and 39 indicate that you tend to offer an intermediate or average level of encouragement to others, while a score of 27 or below indicates that you tend to provide others with low to very low levels of encouragement when interacting with them.

I encourage you to respect others and live a God – focused life.

Use the message incorporated in the following poem entitled "Show Them" to assist you in doing God's will and dealing with environmental demands.

SHOW THEM

When they say that
You cannot succeed. Show them that you
Are the crop; not the weed.

Don't let them push
You around.
Show them that you
Can stand your own ground.

When they try to put
You down.
Show them that you
Are worthy, capable and sound.

Stand straight
And tall.
Show them you
Are strong and will not fall.

When they treat you with little respect.
Show them that you
Can be firm, steady and erect.

Learn how to work
And plan.
Show them that you
Are as good as your fellow man.

James Battle (1995)

THEY SAID

Many things that people say cannot be done can be...

For instance:

1. They said, that humans couldn't run a four-minute mile; then along came a person named Roger Bannister.

2. They said, that Blacks couldn't box; then along came a person named Jack Johnson.

3. They said, that the blind couldn't lead productive lives; then along came a person named Helen Keller.

4. They said, that Blacks couldn't play major league baseball; then along came a person named Jackie Robinson.

5. They said, Gretzky couldn't play big league hockey because he was too small.

6. They said, that Blacks couldn't succeed in professional golf; then along came a person named Eldrick (Tiger) Woods.

7. They said, that Blacks couldn't succeed in professional tennis; then along came:

- Althea Gibson

- Arthur Ashe

- Venus and Serena Williams

8. They said, that Blacks couldn't succeed in big league hockey; then along came:

- Willie O'Ree

- Grant Fuhr

- Mike Grier

- Georges Larague

- Ansen Carter

- Jarome Iginla

- Ray Emery

9. They said, that Aboriginals couldn't play big league sports; then came along a person named

Jim Thorpe.

10. They said, that Blacks couldn't succeed as big league coaches, then along came:

- Bill Russell

a) Who won national basketball titles while serving as a player and coach.

- Cito Gaston

b) Who won back to back world series while managing The Toronto Blue Jays Baseball team.

- Michael Clemons

c) Who won the Grey Cup while coaching The Toronto Argonauts Football team.

- Tony Dungy

d) Who won The Super Bowl while coaching The Indianapolis Colts Football team.

AVOIDING RISK

I'm of the opinion that Christians and non-Christians as well would benefit from striving to become independent thinkers and avoid putting themselves at risk. Support for this position is provided in the following.

BEWARE OF FALSE PROPHETS

Christ said:

"...Beware that no one leads you astray. Many will come in my name and say, "I am He!" and they will lead many astray..." (Mark 13: 1-8).

Acquiring and maintaining autonomy and courage will assist both Christians and non-Christians in their efforts to avoid putting themselves at risk.

AUTONOMY AND COURAGE

Individuals who are vulnerable to social pressure and exploitation put themselves at risk:

1. Autonomy

- Ability of the individual to think for him or herself and do what he or she considers to be best, and

2. Courage

- Ability to face challenges and obstacles without fear

The importance of courage was emphasized by Winston Churchill when he said:

"...Courage is rightly esteemed to be the first of human qualities because it is the quality that guarantees all others."

BENEFIT

I, Battle (2006) encourage individuals to ask themselves questions that address "benefit" prior to making decisions regarding display of behavior:

For instance:

1. How does arguing with others benefit me?

2. How does using illegal drugs benefit me?

3. How does listening to others benefit me?

4. How does practicing safe sex benefit me?

5. How does limiting the amount of alcohol I drink benefit me?

6. How does associating with individuals who are

addicted to alcohol or illegal drugs benefit me?

7. How does co-operating with authority figures benefit me?

8. How does drinking alcohol benefit me?

9. How does obeying rules and regulations established by authorities benefit me?

10. How does learning strategies that help me perform more efficiently at work benefit me?

11. How does employing strategies that assist in avoiding absenteeism and tardiness benefit me at work?

12. How does acquiring knowledge regarding sexually transmitted diseases benefit me?

13. How does being an authentic Christian benefit me?

Supporters of the Christian faith and others can use the knowledge incorporated in the questions listed above to assist themselves in their efforts to do God's will.

In the following, I offer a schematic presentation of James Battle and Associates Ltd. logo, which incorporates three interlocking circles. These circles represent human's mental, physical and spiritual domains.

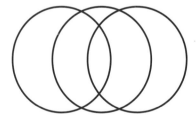

Harmonious integration of these three domains listed above result in humans permitting God to work within them and the promotion of mutual respect, peace and harmony among all peoples.

Readers can use the knowledge incorporated in this section to assist them in their efforts to achieve desired results.

SUMMARY

- Individuals function best when they have effective knowledge.

- Cognitive strategies have demonstrated effectiveness in helping individuals achieve desired results.

- The A-B-C Paradigm can be used to assist individuals in achieving desired results.

- The A-B-C Paradigm is an effective tool and life saving model.

- The Ten Step Countdown is a cognitive procedure that can be used to assist individuals in obtaining personal goals.

- Reflective Listening is a cognitive procedure that can be used to achieve problem resolution.

- Positive Actions are effective tools.

- Mutual Respect is a cognitive strategy that can be used to promote acquisition of desired results.

- Battle proposes an essential Christian commandment that individuals can use to achieve desired results.

- Encouragement is a cognitive strategy that individuals can use to obtain personal goals.

- Individuals can use Battle's poem entitled "Show Them" to facilitate the acquisition of desired results.

- Battle offers a statement entitled "They Said" that individuals can use to achieve desired levels of success.

- Battle encourages individuals to avoid putting themselves at risk.

- Battle proposes that autonomy and courage are important human qualities.

- Battle encourages individuals to live God – focused lives.

Doing God's Will: Using Christian Faith and Psychology

PART IV

Commitment and Service

CHAPTER 4

DISCIPLESHIP

IN THIS CHAPTER I PROVIDE INSIGHTS derived from the tenets of Christian faith and encourage readers to try their very best to avoid being influenced and persuaded by Satan and his cohorts. Also, in this section I list statements of Christian faith and show that all who believe in God and His Son, Jesus Christ can serve as disciples.

I encourage supporters of the Christian faith to consider the knowledge incorporated in the following statement provided by Martin Luther:

> "I trust in him steadfastly, no matter how long he may delay, prescribing neither a goal, nor a time, nor a measure nor a way (for God to respond to me), but leaving all to his divine will in a free, honest, and genuine faith.
>
> If he is almighty, what could I lack that God could not give or do for me?" (L W 43:25).

The insights in these statements make it clear to me that if I maintain steadfast, unswerving faith in God and do His will I will not experience debilitating fear and anxiety.

Insights recorded in I Timothy 2: 1-7 reveals that:

- There is only one true God

- There is only one mediator between God and humans, Jesus Christ

I am of the opinion that:

Christians accept God unswervingly and permit

him to work within them.

Rejection is a powerful emotion that was addressed as follows:

REJECTION OF GOD

Feeling of rejection is the most powerful emotion that humans experience.

God's expression of the importance of rejection is described in Exodus 20: 2-17 recorded in the:

- Ten Commandments when our father said

- I the Lord your God is a jealous God

Who will visit iniquity upon those:

- Who hate me

Humans reject God then they refuse to:

- Be faithful

- Do His will

- Permit Him to work within them

- Love Him

Knowledge derived from Christian tenets is provided in the following statement.

POWER OF REJECTION

Fear of rejection is one of the most powerful motivating forces affecting humans.

The power of rejection is vividly illustrated in Matthew, Chapter 27, verse 46 by Christ who said during the ninth hour on the cross:

"...My God; My God; why hast Thou forsaken me?..."

In the following I record a commonly held misconception:

Misconception

- God punishes His children by employing storms, fires, famines, diseases and a wide variety of other disasters.

Fact

- God is a loving parent who only wants what is best for His children.

God and Unconditional Love

God offers all people:

- Unconditional Love

Provided

- Free of cost

Those who accept God's gift of:

- Unconditional love permits Him to
- Work within them

Those who refuse to accept God and His offer of:

- Unconditional love
- Reject Him and refuse to permit Him to:
- Work within them

Those who:

- Reject God
- Will
- Deal with the consequences

Of their

- Behavior

Grace is an important tenet of the Christian faith. I offer my views regarding grace in the following statement:

Grace is a blessing from God. God provides grace for His children whom He loves. Although grace is provided freely, individuals who desire God's grace need to employ the following steps:

Step 1: Expression of shame

Step 2: Genuine expression of remorse

Step 3: Petition for forgiveness

The following is a personal prayer that I have found to be beneficial.

A PERSONAL PRAYER

I pray Dear God, that you give me:

1. The Faith

And the

2. Wisdom

And the

3. Courage to:

Do Your will

And to:

- Live my life

According to the gospel

Provided by:

- My Lord, Jesus Christ

In the following I provide insights regarding my view of the Christian faith.

FAITH IN GOD

Martin Luther stated:

> "I take the risk of placing my confidence only in the one, invisible, inscrutable, and only God, who created heaven and earth and who alone is superior to all creation. Again, I am not terrified by the wickedness of the devil and his cohorts because God is superior to them all..."

I, (*Battle, 2006*) stated that:

- Authentic Christians

Don't have to experience

- Excessive Anxiety

Because

- Our God

Is the only

- True God

Who

- Created Heaven and Earth

And is

- Superior to all creation

And because of this

- We do not have to fear

- Satan and his cohorts

In the following, I provide a list of sins.

SINS AND SINNERS

The following sins have endured the test of time and they continue to be relevant today:

1. Rejection of God
2. Oppressive abusive power
3. Greed
4. Exploitation of others
5. Envy
6. Wickedness
7. Hatred
8. Evilness
9. Rape
10. Incest
11. Murder
12. Stealing
13. Jealousy
14. Racism

Humans who commit the sins listed above are:

- Unfaithful individuals

Who

- Refuse to

Let

- God work
- Within Them

I share my views regarding the severity of human sins as follows:

HIERARCHY OF SINS

In the following list, I chronicle the Ten Most Serious Sins in descending order with number one representing the most serious Sin and number Ten, the least serious Sin.

1. Rejection of God and His son Jesus Christ

2. Hatred of what Jesus Christ describes as good

3. Deliberately killing another human being

4. Racism

5. Greed

6. Deliberately using false gospels to manipulate others.

7. Using power to exploit others

8. Selfishness

9. Display of evilness while interacting with fellow human beings

10. Lack of Caring and Respect for fellow humans

In the following statement, I present my view regarding racism and racist acts.

RACISM AND SIN

I, (*Battle*) have always felt that being racist was:

- Immoral

And an indication of:

- Stupidity

- Ignorance:

And

- Emotional Disturbance

I am of the opinion that:

- Individuals who display racist acts

Are:

- Committing serious sins

UNDERSTANDING SIN

Most Christian denominations adhere to the position that all humans are sinners, due to the behavior of Adam and Eve in the Garden of Eden. However, I am of the opinion that all humans are sinners because none of us are perfect. It is however important to understand that although all humans are sinners, some of us commit more serious sins than others and some of us sin more frequently. Thus, I am of the opinion that sins, like most constructs can be placed on a continuum ranging from a very low level of seriousness on one end to a very high level of seriousness on the other end. In the following figure, we provide an illustration to show levels of seriousness of sins.

Figure 4:1 Levels of Seriousness of Sin

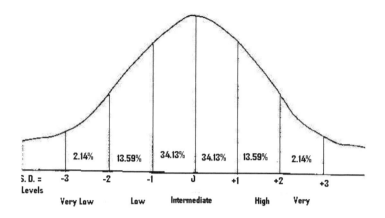

| 2.14% | 13.59% | 34.13% | 34.13% | 13.59% | 2.14% |

| S. D. = Levels | -3 | -2 | -1 | 0 | +1 | +2 | +3 |

| | Very Low | Low | Intermediate | High | Very |

The levels depicted in Figure 4:1, ranging from very low on one end of our continuum to very high on the other end shows that we are all sinners. Thus, because of this, if we desire to rid ourselves of sin, we need to petition God, through prayer asking for forgiveness.

Irrational Fear: A Major Factor in Emotional Disturbance

In my book entitled "Overcoming Racism And Achieving Success", I said:

> "...Racism, in my view is a symptom of emotional disturbance which is due to irrational fear of the individual or group that the racist thoughts and actions are directed towards..."

Although the majority of humans are not racist, a significant proportion of us experience some degree of irrational fear which results in a variety of adjustment problems including:

- Irrational thinking
- Pseudo-self-esteem

- Low self-esteem
- Depression
- Excessive anxiety
- Fewer success experiences
- Diminish goal attainment
- Excessive worry about what others think
- Shame
- Display of self-defeating behavior

Irrational Thinking and Self-Defeat

Albert Ellis the developer of Rational-Emotive Therapy cites the following irrational ideas that he proposed lead to the display of self-defeating behavior.

Irrational Idea No. 1

The idea that it is a dire necessity for an adult human being to be loved or approved by virtually every significant other person in his community.

Irrational Idea No. 2

The idea that one should be thoroughly competent, adequate, and achieving in all possible respects if one is to consider one-self worthwhile.

Irrational Idea No. 3

The idea that certain people are bad, wicked, or villainous and that they should be severely blamed and punished for their villainy.

Irrational Idea No. 4

The idea that it is awful and catastrophic when things are not the way one would very much like them to be.

Irrational Idea No. 5

The idea that human unhappiness is externally caused and that people have little or no ability to control their sorrows and disturbances.

Irrational Idea No. 6

The idea that if something is or may be dangerous or fearsome one should be terribly concerned about it, and should keep dwelling on the possibility of it occurring.

Irrational Idea No. 7

The idea that it is easier to avoid than to face certain life difficulties and self-responsibilities.

Irrational Idea No. 8

The idea that one should be dependent on others and need someone stronger than oneself on whom to rely.

Irrational Idea No. 9

The idea that one's past history is an all important determiner of one's present behavior and that because something once strongly affected one' s life, it should indefinitely have a similar effect.

Irrational Idea No. 10

The idea that one should become quite upset over other people's problems and disturbances.

Irrational Idea No. 11

The idea that there is invariably a right, precise and perfect solution to human problems and that it is catastrophic if this perfect solution is not found.

Irrational Idea No. 12

The idea that one has virtually no control over one's emotions and that one cannot help feeling certain things.

DEALING WITH ANXIETY AND FEARS

I am of the opinion (*Battle, 2007*) that individuals can use the effective knowledge incorporated in the following statement by Martin Luther to assist themselves in their efforts to diminish symptoms of anxiety and overcome fear while striving to do God's will:

> "...only a faith that ventures everything in life and in death on what is said (in scripture) of God makes a person a Christian and obtains all he desires from God. No corrupt or hypocritical heart can have such a faith, this is a living faith as the first commandment demands"

> "I am your God; you shall have no other Gods..."

UNDERSTANDING AND DEALING WITH ANXIETY

Anxiety is a wide spread condition characterized by symptoms such as nervousness, tenseness, and sleep disturbance.

Although statistics reported by psychologists vary, they generally indicate that a significant proportion of individuals residing in our contemporary society experience excessive anxiety. Some of these experiencing individuals employ personas in their efforts to deal with these emotionally charged states.

THE PERSONA

The persona is the mask, which we present to others. It is a protective façade, which conceals the individual's "true" or "inner" nature. Jung proposed that the persona is needed because individuals have to play many roles as they interact with others. Jung described the persona in the following fashion:

> The persona is a compromise between individual and society as to what a man should appear to be like "...putting on official airs" or "playing a role..." Society expects, and indeed must expect, every individual to play the part assigned to him

as perfectly as possible. Each must stand at his post; here a cobbler, there a poet. No man is expected to be both. Nor is it advisable to be both, for that would be odd. Such a man would be different from the other people; not quite reliable. In the academic world he would be a dilettante; in politics an unpredictable quantity; in religion a free thinker. In short, he would always be suspected of unreliability and incompetence because society is persuaded that only the cobbler who is not a poet can supply workmanlike shoes (*1972, pp 192-193*).

The persona is vividly illustrated if the following poem entitled "Masks":

MASKS

Don't be fooled by the face I wear, for I wear a thousand masks.
And none of them are me. Don't be fooled.
For God's sake, don't be fooled.

I give you the impression that I'm secure,
that confidence is my name
and coolness my game, and that I need no one.
But don't believe me.

Beneath dwells the real me in confusion, in loneliness, in fear.
That's why I create a mask to hide behind, to shield me from the
glance that knows.

But, such a glance is precisely my salvation.
That is, if it is followed by acceptance, if it is followed by love.
It's the only thing that can liberate me from my own self-built prison
walls.

I'm afraid that deep down I'm nothing and that
I'm just no good,
And that you will see this and reject me.

And so begins the parade of masks
I idly chatter to you. I tell you everything that's really nothing,
and nothing of what's everything, of what's crying within me.

Please listen carefully and try to hear what I' m NOT saying,
I'd really like to be genuine and spontaneous, and ME.
But you got to help me,
You've got to hold out your hand.

Each time you're kind, and gentle, and encouraging,
Each time you try to understand because you really care
My heart begins to grow wings. Very feeble wings, but wings.

With your sensitivity and sympathy, and your
powerful understanding
you alone can release me from my shallow
world of uncertainty.
It will not be easy for you.

The nearer you approach me, the blinder I may strike back,
But, I'm told that love is stronger than strong walls,
and in this lies my hope.
My only hope.

Please try to beat down these walls with firm hands,
But gentle hands, for a child is very sensitive.

Who am I, you may wonder, I am every man you meet, and every
woman you meet.
And I am YOU, also.

Author Unknown

Authentic Christians typically experience lower levels of anxiety and fear. Their faith and willingness to let God work within them enable them to achieve this result.

I am of the opinion that the following can be incorporated in daily routines to assist in doing God's will.

FAITH, HOPE, PERSEVERANCE

Faith is:

- Confidence in someone or something

Hope is:

- Expectation of something desired

Perseverance is:

- To persist in spite of obstacles

With faith in God and His son Jesus Christ, there is ever lasting:

- Hope
- Perseverance

With these you can obtain your:

- Goals
- Desired levels of success

Data derived from Canada's 2001 census survey indicate that 80 percent of Canadians identify themselves as being Christians.

USING CHRISTIAN FAITH TO DEAL WITH CHALLENGES AND OVERCOME OBSTACLES: THE TONY DUNGY STORY

Tony Dungy, the head coach of The Indianapolis Colts Football Team, is a Christian who has experienced many loses in a fairly brief period of time. These include:

- Losing key playoff games to opponents
- Being fired by The Tampa Bay Buccaneers despite his winning record

- Seeing the team that he built winning The Super Bowl, the first season after he was fired

- Losing his eighteen year old son to suicide in 2006

- Making the decision to donate his son's organs for transplants

- Receiving a letter thanking him and his family for donated organs that provided sight for a previously blind individual

- Winning The Super Bowl in 2007, while coaching the Indianapolis Colts Football Team.

In the following, I present some characteristics of authentic Christians.

AUTHENTIC CHRISTIANS

Authentic Christians are genuine males and females who:

- Do not mask their imperfections

- Do not seek praise from others

- Do not employ flattery

- Respect self and others

- Live their lives in concert with the gospel provided by Jesus Christ

Authentic Christians Also:

- Value the worth of human lives

- Recognize the inherent worth of others

- Treat others with respect

- Realize that all humans are brothers and sisters of equal worth

- Realize that God is God of all

- Love God and Christ

- Practice and maintain their faith in God and Christ

- Realize that God's love for humans is unconditional

- Realize that only God is perfect

- Are not racist.

I'm of the opinion that only authentic Christians will reside in heaven and experience an eternity of peace. I take this position because the first of the oldest version of the Ten Commandments reads:

> "I am the Lord your God, who brought you out of the land of Egypt, out of the house of bondage."
>
> "You shall have no other Gods before Me."
>
> "You shall not make for yourself a graven image, or any likeness of what is in heaven above or in the earth beneath or in the water under the earth."
>
> "You shall not worship them or serve them; for I, the Lord your God, am a jealous God, visiting the iniquity of the fathers on the children, to the third and the fourth generations of those who hate Me, but showing steadfast love to thousands, of those who love Me and keep My commandments."

Source: Exodus 20: 2-17

Some views regarding Christ and authentic Christians are presented in the following statement:

CHRIST AND AUTHENTIC CHRISTIANS

Authentic (real; genuine) Christians believe that everything worthwhile comes from Jesus; from His:

- Incarnation

- Teachings

- Ministry

- Healing

- Crucifixion

- Atonement of sins

- Defeat of death

USING "IF" STATEMENTS TO PROMOTE AUTHENTIC CHRISTIAN VALUES

J. Battle (2005) propose that you can use "if" statements such as the following to strengthen beliefs and increase the probability of living your life in a fashion that is in concert with the gospel, provided by Jesus Christ, Lord and Savior. For example:

1. If greed is in concert with the gospel provided by Jesus Christ, I will support it.

2. If evilness is in concert with the gospel provided by Jesus Christ, I will support it.

3. If kindness is in concert with the gospel provided by Jesus Christ, I will support it.

4. If murder is in concert with the gospel provided by Jesus Christ, I will support it.

5. If peace and harmony is in concert with the gospel provided by Jesus Christ, I will support it.

6. If selfishness is in concert with the gospel provided by Jesus Christ, I will support it.

7. If love is in concert with the gospel provided by Jesus Christ, I will support it.

8. If the behavior displayed by an individual is in

concert with the gospel provided by Jesus Christ, I will support him or her.

9. If persecution of the innocent is in concert with the gospel provided by Jesus Christ, I will support the action.

10. If pride is in concert with the gospel provided by Jesus Christ, I will support the disposition.

11. If slander is in concert with the gospel provided by Jesus Christ, I will support it.

12. If righteousness is in concert with the gospel provided by Jesus Christ, I will support it.

13. If worshipping God is in concert with the gospel provided by Jesus Christ, I will support it.

14. If an eye for an eye, a tooth for a tooth is in concert with the gospel provided by Jesus Christ, I will support this position.

15. If revenge is in concert with the gospel provided by Jesus Christ, I will support this behavior.

16. If hatred is in concert with the gospel provided by Jesus Christ, I will support this disposition.

17. If dishonesty is in concert with the gospel provided by Jesus Christ, I will support this behavior.

18. If deceit is in concert with the gospel provided by Jesus Christ, I will support this behavior.

19. If belief in the Father, Son, and Holy Spirit is in concert with the gospel provided by Jesus Christ, I will support it.

20. If negative racial prejudice is in concert with the gospel provided by Jesus Christ, I will support

this disposition.

In the following, I offer a personal opinion.

PERSONAL OPINION

I am of the opinion (*Battle 2006*) that:

1. Everything good that I produce:

Is due to

- God working within one

And that

2. Everything Bad that I produce:

Is due to

- My refusal to let God work within me.

The following statement is provided to share some personal views.

GOD, HUMANS, AND HELL

God does not sentence people to hell

However

- He intervenes only on rare occasions to stop Satan from sentencing sinners to hell

- Sinners are those individuals who had the opportunity to know the true God and His son, Jesus Christ

But

- Rejected God and Christ

And

- Displayed evilness while interacting with fellow humans

Evilness is characterized by:

- Greed
- Selfishness
- Lack of caring and respect for fellow humans
- Using power to exploit others
- Deliberately using gospels to manipulate others
- Hatred of what Jesus Christ described as good

In the following, I share my views regarding what happens to humans when they die.

WHEN HUMANS DIE

When humans die, the souls of the:

- Cohorts of Satan go immediately to
- Hell

When Christ returns to earth to:

- Judge the living and the dead, the cohorts of Satan will
- Return to earth and reclaim their bodies

And

- Return to hell

To

- Suffer for an eternity

When

- Authentic Christians die

Their souls go

- Immediately

To Heaven

When Christ returns to earth to

- Judge the living and the dead, faithful Christians will:

- Return to earth

And

- Reclaim their bodies

And

- Return to heaven

To

- Live in peace

For an

- Eternity

In the following statement, I share some of my views and insights.

DEATH HEAVEN AND HELL

Human death is a process in which living ceases, the soul exits and the body decay.

Hell is a place created by Satan and occupied by sinners who have to endure severe and persistent:

- Pain

- Fear

- Torment

- Despondency

- Sadness

Heaven is a place created by God and occupied by Authentic Christians who experience persistent:

- Happiness
- Contentment
- Gratitude
- Joy
- Elation

The following statement serves as a cue reminding me to maintain determination to achieve the desired result of doing God's will.

REMEMBER

Remember that they:

- Belittled Him
- Despised Him
- Refused to esteem Him
- Rejected Him

And He didn't resist

Remember that they:

- Crucified Him
- Killed Him

Remember that, although He could have:

- Destroyed his adversaries

He didn't

- Resist

Rather, He said

- Father, forgive them for they do not know what they are doing

Remember that the Apostles said:

- There he goes the lamb of God who comes to take away the sins of the world

Remember that God replied:

- This is My Son my beloved whom I love;

- With Him I am well pleased

Remember that:

- He died for all of us

I share my views regarding God's commandments and human interaction in the following statement.

COMMANDMENTS AND HUMAN INTERACTION

J. Battle, (*1993, 1994, 1995*) propose that the interactive process is the most important variable affecting human relations. Support for this position is provided by the Ten Commandments. The first three of the ten:

Instruct humans to:

- Love God

- Have and maintain faith in God

- And do

- God's will

The remaining seven are about:

- Our relationship with others (see Chapter 2)

J. Battle (2006) propose that consideration of self-esteem, mutual respect and encouragement promote positive relationships among humans.

CONSIDERATION OF SELF-ESTEEM

When humans consider the self-esteem of others they make concerted efforts to ensure that the behavior that they emit does not exert a negative effect on the self-esteem of those that they are interacting with.

MUTUAL RESPECT

When humans provide mutual respect to others they make it clear to them that they feel that they just as good as they are and that they have the same rights and responsibilities.

ENCOURAGEMENT

When we encourage others, we emphasize the positive aspects of their behavior rather than the negative aspects. That is, when we encourage others, we minimize the importance of their mistakes while recognizing their assets and strengths.

FORGIVENESS

Forgiveness is a major tenet of the Christian faith. The need of forgiveness was expressed by the author of The Lord's Prayer, Who said:

> "...forgive us our trespasses as we forgive those that trespass against us..."

> As humans, we offer forgiveness to others when we genuinely love, respect and encourage them. The most important of these is love, which was expressed by Christ when He said "....a new commandment I give you, that you love one another" (John 13:34) (*Battle, 1990, Misconceptions Regarding Self-Esteem, page 129*).

Ultimate, everlasting forgiveness is provided by God through His son Jesus Christ, mediator between heaven and earth and founder of the Christian Church. Christ supporters adhere to the position that "He will come again to judge the living and the dead." (Apostle's Creed)" The time of Christ's return is known only by the Father.

In the following, we offer empirically derived, relevant insights regarding the importance of forgiveness.

FORGIVENESS AND HEALTH

Research findings indicate that individuals who are more forgiving of others report:

- Higher levels of satisfaction with their own lives

  And rate their

- Health levels higher

  Than those who

  Can't forgive

Research findings also indicate that forgiveness is associated with:

- Low blood pressure
- Less chronic back pain
- Lower levels of depression
- Better rehabilitation results for spinal cord injured patients

Research findings indicate that un-forgiveness (not being able to forgive) is associated with:

- Anger
- And is linked to mortality rates including:
- Death from heart disease

J. Battle (*2006*) propose that it is not the:

- Verbalizing of forgiveness by the victim that has

The:

- Positive therapeutic effects

Rather, it is the:

- Letting go of hostilities towards the

Perpetrator that results in:

- Wellness

In the following statement, I provide additional insights regarding the need of forgiveness.

UNDERSTANDING FORGIVENESS

The Christian Church instructs its members to:

- Forgive

Those who

- Exploit them

However, I (*Battle, 2006*) propose that:

- Perpetrators need to
- Petition God

And ask for

- Forgiveness

Because I am of the opinion that only

- God can forgive the sins of humans

Support for the position listed above is provided by:

- Jesus Christ
- When He said

- Father forgive them because

- They do not know what they are doing

Additional support for the position presented above is provided in the following passage:

> "...and every priest stands day after day at His service offering again and again the same sacrifices that can never take away sins..."

(Hebrews 10: 11-14)

Brian Jayawardhana, a Catholic priest and certified psychologist offers the following regarding forgiveness:

> "...In order for individuals to be forgiven they need to make a genuine change in their behavior..."

A significant proportion of individuals residing in our contemporary society tend to deny and provide justification for the "bad" behavior of those they prefer. However, I am of the opinion that, supporters of the Christian faith need to recognize both "good" and "bad" behavior and when necessary avoid interacting with those who display evil behavior. Support for this position is provided in the following passage "...if your brother sins against you, go show him his fault, just between the two of you. If he listens to you, you have won your brother over, but if he will not listen, take one or two others along, as that every matter may be established by testimony of two or three witnesses. If he refuses to listen to them, tell it to the church; and if he refuses to listen even to the church, treat him as you would a pagan or a tax collector." (Matthew 18: 15-17)

DEALING WITH BEHAVIOR

God's eighth commandment is:

"...you shall not bear false witness against your neighbour."

It is important however, that:

- Humans recognize behavior displayed by
- Their counterparts whether it is
- Good

Or

- Bad

Whether it

- Contributes to the well being of others

Or

- Exploit them

And

- Impede their progress

CHRISTIAN FAITH AND WELLNESS

Although findings derived from research studies addressing the relationship between Christian faith and recovery from illnesses are mixed, findings of a recent study (2007), conducted by Dr. Salvatora Giaquinto reported data which indicate that strong religious and spiritual beliefs can protect stroke patients from emotional distress. Findings of this study provide support for my position which is that:

"...Doing God's will generally result in more satisfactorily mental, physical, and spiritual levels of adjustment..."

Knowing this can be used as encouragement to assist you in your effort to persevere and do God's will.

I state my belief that God called me to serve others in the following statement:

ANSWERING GOD'S CALL

I believe that God called me to:

- Serve others

However, I didn't realize this until

- 1998 when I drove a student home,

And she said

- Dr. Battle, you are my:
- Angel
- Who came to
- Save me

Without your help

- I would not be
- Alive today

When I attended university at Southern Illinois as an undergraduate, I drove a school bus to make spending money. Although I was a football player on full scholarship, I needed spending money because my mother died when I was eleven years old and my father passed away when I was a nineteen-year-old seaman in the American Navy. Subsequent to their death, I did not receive any financial assistance from any one in my family. Because of this, driving the bus provided me money that I used to purchase clothes and other products. While serving as a part time bus driver, I drove students majoring in psychology on field trips to a nearby mental hospital. While on these trips, I had the opportunity to observe individuals with severe mental illnesses that required hospitalization. Also, while serving as a driver during my junior year at university I made the commitment to become a psychologist and serve individuals experiencing severe mental illnesses. In 1972, I earned my doctor's degree, and in 2004, God answered my prayers when the individuals with severe mental health problems moved to our facility.

STRENGTHENING FAMILIES: USING CHRISTIAN FAITH AND COMMITMENT

In 1996, my wife Dorothy and I was blessed with the privilege of operating a program entitled "Strengthening Black Families: Overcoming Racism And Achieving Success In Mainstream Society." The program was intended to provide black parents and their children the tools they need to achieve success in mainstream society. Parents and their children aged 6 through 16 years who participated in the program, were provided forty-two hours of instruction simultaneously, in twenty-one class periods at the same location.

During the first 90 minutes of each 120-minute session, parents were taught strategies that they could use to enhance their children's self-esteem, achievement and well-being and assist their offspring in adjusting to environmental demands. Also, during these periods parents were taught strategies they could use to enhance their own self-esteem, success experiences and well-being. During this same period, participating children were taught strategies intended to assist them in developing their full potential and adjusting more effectively to environmental demands. In addition, during this period, the children were provided remedial instruction in reading, spelling and arithmetic intended to enhance their academic achievement levels.

During the last 30-minute period of each session, parents and their children met together as one combined group for black history instruction. The goals of the program for parents and their children were to:

- Provide participating parents and children effective tools to increase the probability of them acquiring self-sufficiency and benefiting from every aspect of society.

- Provide black parents and their children strategies that will enable them to interact effectively in all sectors of their community

- Provide parents and their children assessments intended to enable them to gain insights regarding racial relations

- Provide black parents and their children the tools they need to overcome racism and achieve success

- Provide black families with effective strategies that promote co-operation and racial harmony among all groups.

- Provide children and youth aged 6 to 16 years experiences to assist them in achieving success at school and in the community

RESULTS

All individuals were administered a battery of instruments during pre and post tests to determine the effects that the program had on participants. Boys and girls were administered *The Culture-Free Self-Esteem Inventory For Children, Form A*; the spelling and arithmetic portions of *The Wide Range Achievement Test-Revised, 3*, and the vocabulary portion of *The Gates MacGinite Reading Test* during pre-tests that occurred shortly after the program commenced during November,1996 and on a second occasion when the program ended during April,

1997. Participating parents were administered *The Culture-Free Self-Esteem Inventory for Adults, Form AD, and The Race Relations Inventory* during the same periods.

Results derived from the analysis of pre and post-test scores indicate that participating children and their parents acquired the empowerment needed to assist them in achieving success in spite of the negative effects of racism. The children experienced positive shifts in their self-esteem, reading, spelling, and arithmetic scores. Their parents experienced positive gains in their self-esteem and race relations scores.

Subsequent to the project described above, we operated another program entitled "Strengthening Black And Aboriginal Families: Achieving Success In Mainstream Society." In this project, we provided participants the same experiences described in our 1996 program, and in addition, taught both black and aboriginal history. The results achieved in this project were basically identical to those reported in the 1996 initiative.

My wife and I continue to commit ourselves to serving aboriginal children, youth and adults at our Self-Esteem Institute of Canada, in Edmonton, Alberta and on site in communities in other regions of Canada.

I provide a program of social services instruction for the individuals with severe mental illnesses who live in our forty unit housing facility. The majority of residents who participate in our social services program are individuals with diagnoses of schizophrenia. I make it very clear to each resident that I am of the opinion that they are worthy and that they can do things. My views regarding their worth are stated in the following that I incorporate in my presentations and give copies to participants:

A message from Dr. B.,

> Always remember that
> You are
> Just as good as
> Anyone else
> And that
> You can do things.

Also, during my presentations, I tell participants about Clifford Beers, an American proponent of the socio-cultural view who had a significant impact on the mental health movement while a patient himself. His views were delineated in his classic manuscript entitled "A Mind That Found Itself." This book served as a catalyst which enabled Beers to initiate his national crusade of reforms for mental patients. The mental hygiene movement initiated by Beers spread rapidly throughout the United States, Europe and eventually the world. Beers' influence and innovative ideas provided the base from which mental hygiene programs nationally and internationally received their genesis.

Beers is considered by many to be the father of the modern mental hygiene movement. Beers experienced a severe adjustment failure and as a consequence was hospitalized. As a patient, he attempted on numerous occasions to get hospital officials to improve the conditions of the hospital. However, he was unsuccessful, and as a consequence, he smuggled letters out to state officials describing the conditions in the hospital. These letters prompted state officials to institute legislation, which subsequently improved the conditions in mental institutions. Upon release, Beers wrote, "A Mind That Found Itself" and intensified his reform activities.

Satan and his cohorts consistently persist in their

efforts to convince authentic Christians and other Christians as well, to reject God and His son Jesus Christ. Because of this, it is important that all Christians recognize their adversaries and avoid exploitation and manipulation.

The insights presented in this chapter were inspired by my desire to share with others personal beliefs and positions regarding commitment and service, derived from documents that I have found to be beneficial in assisting me in my efforts to do God's will.

SUMMARY

- Battle proposes that all humans are brothers and sisters of equal worth.

- Authentic Christians believe that God is within each human.

- Rejection is a powerful motivational force-affecting humans.

- Battle asserts that God loves all humans unconditionally.

- God provides grace for His children whom He loves.

- Battle offers a personal prayer that he has found to be beneficial.

- Martin Luther proposed that authentic Christians maintain faith, and confidence in God.

- Battle proposes that sins and sinners have endured the test of time and continue to be relevant today.

- Battle proposes that racism and racist acts are serious sins.

- Battle encourages individuals to maintain faith, hope, and perseverance in their efforts to achieve desired results.

- Battle proposes that racism is a symptom of emotional disturbance.

- Irrational ideas result in adjustment problems.

- Irrational ideas lead to the display of self-defeating behavior.

- Battle proposes that effective knowledge can be

used to diminish symptoms of anxiety.

• Battle proposes that authentic Christians are genuine males and females who value the worth of human lives.

• Battle offers "If" statements that individuals can use to help them achieve desired results.

• Battle offers his views of the age-old debate of what happens when humans die.

• Battle has found his statement entitled "Remember" to be beneficial to him in his efforts to do God's will.

• Battle proposes that the interactive process is the most important variable affecting human relations.

• Battle proposes that forgiveness is a major tenet of the Christian faith.

• A significant proportion of Canadians report they feel that forgiveness is very important.

• A significant number of Canadians report that they are Christians.

• Battle proposes that it is important that humans be prepared to answer God's call for discipleship.

• Battle used Christian faith and commitment to strengthen families.

PART V

Concluding Remarks

USING COGNITIVE STRATEGIES TO DEAL WITH STRESS AND ACHIEVE GOALS

In the following, I illustrate how I employed cognitive strategies to deal with a stressful situation and achieve desired results.

On the morning of a very important trip, my alarm clock was set to ring at 5 a.m., but because of a power outage it rang at 6:45 a.m. I discovered this at 7 a.m. Because of this, I had only one hour and five minutes to travel forty miles to reach the airport, park my vehicle and board the aircraft. It appeared impossible to accomplish this feat; however, I reminded myself to think positive and employ some of the cognitive strategies that I routinely teach my psychotherapy clients in efforts to accomplish the goal of making my 8:05 a.m. flight. Thus, I very quickly decided to employ the A-B-C Paradigm, initially, then the Ten-Step Count Down Procedure and followed these with Reflective Listening.

The A-B-C Paradigm

The A-B-C Paradigm is an effective strategy that can be used to control arousal and increase the probability of emitting behavior that is self-enhancing rather than self-defeating. Thus, I used this strategy initially because it was important for me to control my levels of arousal and make rational choices.

The Ten-Step Count Down Procedure

The Ten Step Count Down Procedure is a cognitive strategy that can be used to control impulses and maintain optimal levels of arousal. While using this strategy I Counted down from ten to one (e. g. 10, 9, 8, 7, 6, 5, 4, 3, 2, 1) at a rate of about one digit per second and immediately afterwards gave myself a verbal cue (e.g. focus;

relax; stay calm).

Reflective Listening

Reflective Listening is a cognitive strategy that can be used to acquire resolutions to problems and achieve desired results. I employed this strategy in efforts to resolve my problem of leaving home late and achieve the desired result of arriving at the airport "in time" to make my scheduled flight.

CHRONOLOGY

...When I discovered that I had awakened approximately one hour and 45 minutes late, I immediately employed the A-B-C Paradigm and told myself at point "B" not to make myself upset and to do the best that I could to ensure that my actions at "C" yield consequences that were self-enhancing rather than self-defeating. By doing this, I was able to control my levels of arousal. After doing this, I ten stepped it in my efforts to acquire optimal levels of focusing and maintain "appropriate' levels of arousal. Finally, I realized that I needed to achieve resolution to the problem that I was confronted with. Thus, because of this I employed Reflective Listening. The first thing that I did while using Reflective Listening was to explore alternatives regarding; the best route to take to the airport, speed levels, where to park at the airport and what to do when I got inside. The route that I chose to take was the one, which I felt, had less traffic; I drove the route at speeds that exceeded the speed limit and I decided to park right in front of the door leading to the ticket counter of the airline that I was scheduled to take. I also decided to go directly to the ticket counter after parking and search for a luggage attendant who I knew personally. When I arrived at the ticket counter the airline attendant phoned to see if the plane was still at the gate; learning that the plane had not left, she processed my ticket and baggage quickly. During this time, I searched for the luggage attendant that I knew; found him very quickly and gave him my luggage that had been processed by the attendant at the ticket counter, and my keys. I asked him if he would park my vehicle, rush my baggage to the immigration area, and he did. He assured me that he would take care of my requests. The immigration official opened the gate that had been closed and the employees inside processed my identification papers quickly. I made my flight, which left on schedule!

While traveling en-route to my destination, I wrote the following letter:

Manager

Terminal Manager Edmonton Airports
PO Box 9860
Edmonton, Alberta T5J 272

Dear Manager:

The purpose of this correspondence is to thank the entire staff, including American immigration officials for the superb service they provided me which enabled me to make my scheduled flight.

I arrived at the Edmonton International Airport at 7:50 a.m. for my flight, which was scheduled to leave at 8:05 a.m. Immediately upon arrival I parked my car at the departure level in front of the North West Airlines ticket counter and rushed in with my baggage. The attendant who processed my ticket very quickly, arranged for me to proceed through American Immigration. While she was doing this, I yelled for Mr. Eugene Hayes who came to my rescue. I told Eugene about my problem, and he responded without hesitation by taking my bags through immigration directly to the conveyor belt for loading on the plane. He also, upon my request, took my car keys and parked my vehicle in long-term parking. The attendant and immigration officers rushed me through and I was able to make my flight.

Again, I want to take this opportunity to thank all of the people who so graciously provided exemplary services for me, which enabled me to make my scheduled flight. You can phone me at 780-488-1362, or toll free in Canada, at 1-800-463-9144 at any time. In addition, if you like, you can fax me at 780-482-3332, or e-mail me jbattle@telusplanet.net

With Mutual Respect,

James Battle, Ph.D.

PART VI

Remembrance

In the following, I provide an overview of my position regarding the importance of service and mission.

REMEMBRANCE

When I die, I want to be remembered as a
person who cared
who supported others and shared

When I die, I want to
be remembered as a person
who did what was right
who worked hard to make the future bright

When I die, I want to
be remembered as a person who was honest and strong
who had a keen vision
of what was right or wrong

When I die, I want
to be remembered as a person who stood erect
who helped others and
provided all respect

When I die, I want to
be remembered as a person with faith and grace
who accepted the entire human race

When I die, I want to
be remembered as an angel in disguise
who had faith and vision and was wise

When I die, I want to be remembered
as a person who made the journey through
life
without giving into greed, hatred, violence or vice

When I die, I want to
be remembered as a person who was willing to pray
who looked forward to peace and Judgement Day.

James Battle

PART VII

Glossary of Terms and

References

Glossary of Terms

A

ABSENTEEISM: Non-attendance

ABUSE: To humiliate

ACADEMIC SELF-ESTEEM: An individual's perception of his or her ability to succeed academically

ACCOMMODATE: To fit, or harmonize with

ADJUSTMENT: A satisfactory state of functioning

ADULTERY: Voluntary sexual intercourse by a married person with someone who is not the individual's spouse

ADVOCATE: One who supports another

AFFECT: Emotion or mood

AFFECTIVE DISORDERS: Psychological conditions characterized by extremes in moods

AGE: Period of years lived

AGE APPROPRIATE: Display of behavior characteristic of chronological age

AGGRESSION: An attack characterized by display of hostile behavior

ALTRUISM: The principle of doing good for others

AMELIORATE: To make better

ANACHRONISM: Something out of keeping with the time

ANCIENT: Of time in the past belonging to the early history of the world

ANGEL: Messenger of God

ANGER: An emotional state, which is characterized by hostile feelings

ANNIHILATE: To destroy

ANXIETY DISORDER: A condition characterized by irrational apprehension

APOSTLE: An advocate, crusader, messenger, teacher, and supporter. Also, a person selected and sent on a special mission

APOSTLE'S CREED: An ancient statement of belief in the Christian doctrine

ARDENT: Intense or passionate feelings

ASCEND: To soar up, float up, fly up

ASSERTIVENESS: Tendency or disposition to do things with confidence

ASSESSMENT: Test or Estimate

AUTHENTIC: Real, genuine

AUTHENTIC LIFESTYLE: One that is in concert with the morals, principles and values of the experiencing person

AUTONOMY: Ability of the individual to think for him or herself and do what he or she considers to be best

B

BAPTIZE: To dip a person into water or pour or sprinkle water over him as a symbol of admission into christening for a specific Christian church

BAPTISMAL CREED: The Apostle's Creed or Nicene Creed

BARRIER: Something that impedes

BEGOTTEN: To beget, to be the father or sire of, procreate, to bring into being

BEHAVIOR: Conduct

BEHAVIOR CONTROL: Control of conduct

BEHAVIOR MODIFICATION: A form of therapy, utilizing learning principles, and focuses on the amelioration of symptoms or overt actions rather than subjective feelings or unconscious processes

BELIEF: An opinion or disposition that an individual possess which he or she considers to be true

BIAS: A one sided inclination

BIRTH ORDER: Ordinal position of birth

BONDAGE: Subjection to some force, influence or compulsion

C

CATHARSIS: To purify, release or alleviate
CATECHISM: Instruction
CATHOLIC CHURCH: The universal church headed by a pope
CHALLENGE: Condition to overcome
CHRIST: The Messiah whose appearance is prophesied in the Old Testament
CHRISTIAN: Follower of Christ
CHRISTIAN ERA: The period beginning with the birth of Christ
CLERK: An employee who assists an employer
COGNITION: The process of thinking and perceiving
COGNITIVE: The mental process or faculty of knowing
COGNITIVE DISSONANCE: The tendency to maintain psychological consistency and stability in spite of information which is contrary to, or disapproves our assumptions or beliefs
COGNITIVE PSYCHOTHERAPY: Approach that emphasizes rational thinking
COHORT: An associate, colleague, or supporter
COMMANDMENT: An authoritative command or order
COMMITMENT: Dedication to an undertaking
COMMUNION: Participating in the Eucharist, sacrament
COMPASSION: Sorrow for the sufferings or trouble of another or others, accompanied by an urge to help
COMPUTER TRAINING: Instruction in the operation and application of computers
CONCISE: Brief and to the point
CONCEIVE: To create
CONCURRENT: Occurring at the same time, existing together

CONDEMN: To pass an adverse judgment

CONDITION: Anything essential to the existence or occurrence of something else

CONDITIONAL LOVE: Love that is contingent on behavior

CONDUCT DISORDERS: Disorders of childhood and adolescence that violate the rights of others

CONFESSION: An acknowledgement, admission of guilt

CONGREGATION: An assembly or gathering of people or things

CONQUER: To get possession or control

CONSCIENCE: Personal or subjective judgment regarding what is right or wrong

CONSANGUINITY: Relationship by descent from the same ancestor; blood relationship

CONTROL: To regulate or restrain

CONSULTANT: One who provides advice and assistance

CONTRACTOR: Person who agrees to deliver services

CONVERSION REACTION: Condition in which anxiety is converted into physical symptoms

COPING STRATEGIES: Strategies used to promote adjustment and reduce stress

CORRELATION: The tendency of certain arrays of frequency distributions to be positively, negatively, or not at all associated

COVET: To ardently want something that belongs to another

COVETOUSNESS: The act of wanting something that belongs to another

CREDIBILITY: Doing what one promises to do

CREED: A brief statement of religious belief

CRUCIFIED: To be put to death

CUE: A stimulus that directs one's actions

D

DEATH: Permanent ending of all life in a person, animal or plant

DECALOGUE: Ten Commandments

DEIFY: To make divine, look up upon or worship, glorify, exalt, idolize, or adore in an extreme way

DEITY: The state of being God, the supreme spiritual being

DEFENSE MECHANISM: Mechanism employed by the ego as a defense against anxiety and threat

DELUSION: A belief contrary to reality, which persists in spite of evidence which proves it false

DELUSION OF PERSECUTION: False belief that others are out to harm one

DEMONOLOGY: The belief that holds that mental disorders are due to demonistic possession

DENIAL: Defense mechanism employed by the ego as a defense against anxiety and threat

DEPRESSION: An emotional disorder characterized by difficulties concentrating or despondent mood, mood disorder characterized by feelings of sadness

DESCEND: To sink or plunge; to move from a higher level to a lower one

DESPISE: To condemn, dislike and disdain another

DESTRUCTION: To pull down, overthrow or decimate

DEVASTATE: To ravage or destroy

DEVELOPMENT: Growth through maturity

DEVIL: Satan, or evil spirit or very wicked person

DISCIPLE: Follower of a teacher, a school of religion

DISPLACEMENT: Defense mechanism in which psychic energy is re-channeled, or redirected from one object, person or situation to another

DISSONANCE: Incompatible attitudes or emotions

DYSFUNCTION: Deviant or abnormal functioning

E

EARTH: The planet that we live on, a terrestrial globe

EDUCATION: The action or process of educating or being educated

EGO: Term employed by intra-psychic or Freudian theorists to refer to the dimension of the personality that mediates between the id and superego

EGO IDEAL: One's views regarding what he feels he ought to be

EGO STRENGTH: The ability of the individual to cope with the demands of his or her environment

EMINENT: Rising above others

EMIT: To discharge, vent or send out

EMOTION: A neurophysiological reaction to impending stimuli

EMPIRICAL: Relying and based solely on experiment and observation rather than theory

EMPLOYMENT: Work

EMPLOYER: One who employs

EMPLOYMENT TRAINING: Training that prepares participants for work

ENCOURAGEMENT: To inspire, spur and support another

ENDOGENOUS: Originating within the individual

ENVY: Dislike towards another who has something that one desires

EPITAPH: An inscription on a tomb or gravestone

ETERNAL: Never stopping, always going on, existing through all time

ETERNITY: Continuance of time without end

EUCHARIST: Holy Communion

EVIL: That which is not good and produces pain

EXORCISM: Ancient procedure or removing demonic spirits from the minds of humans

EXOGENOUS: Originating outside the organism

EXPLOITATION: To take advantage of

EXTINCTION: Elimination of an acquired response

F

FALSE: Not true, the act of deceiving
FAMILIAL: Pertaining to characteristics that appear to occur more frequently among particular families
FAMILY: A group of descendants of common ancestors
FORGIVE: To absolve, acquit, pardon
FORGIVENESS: Inclination to forgive, or pardon
FUNDAMENTAL NEEDS: Essential needs
FACILITATOR: Person who promotes, guides, and supports
FULFILL: To carry out something promised, expected or predicted

G

GENERAL SELF-ESTEEM: An individual's general perception of his or her worth
GENERATION: The act or process of producing off-spring
GENERALIZATION: The process of transferring the learning acquired in a given situation to another situation
GOAL: Desired result
GOD: The Supreme Being
GRACE: The unmerited love and favor that God provides humans
GRAVE: A hole in the ground in which to bury a dead body
GRAVEN IMAGE: An idol

H

HALLOW: To make holy or sacred

HARMONY: In agreement
HEAVEN: Where God and His angels reside
HOLY: Blessed, divine, righteous
HOLY SPIRIT: The Spirit of God; the third person of the Christian Trinity
HOMAGE: Anything given to show the reverence, honor, or respect
HOMEOSTASIS: Maintaining optimal constancy or equilibrium in psychological process
HOPE: Expectation of something desired

I

ID: The dimension of personality, according to intra-psychic or Freudian theorists, which is the source of primitive impulses
IDOLATRY: Worship of, idols, excessive devotion to or reverence for some person or thing
IMMACULATE: Perfectly clean, without spot or stain
IMPEDE: To block
INCARNATION: Endowment with a human body
INCONGRUENCE: Not accordant; not fitting together
INIQUITY: Wickedness, unjust, lack of righteousness, or justice
INSCRUTABLE: Not easily understood, completely obscure or mysterious
INSIGHT: Increasing awareness and understanding of meaningful relationships
INSTINCT: Inherited disposition that is characteristic of all members of a given species
INTELLIGENCE: The ability to adapt to environmental demands
INTELLIGENCE QUOTIENT: A score derived from performance on standardized tests of intelligence commonly referred to as IQ
INVIOLABLE: Not to be violated, profaned, or injured

INTROJECT: Taking in someone's personality dispositions

J

JESUS CHRIST: Son of God, founder of the Christian faith

K

KINGDOM: The spiritual realm of God, a government or country headed by a king, or queen or monarchy

L

LABILE: Pertaining to instability marked by mood changes
LATENT: A disposition that is dormant or inactive
LIBIDO: The portion of the ID that is basically sexual in nature
LIFE SKILLS: Skills for living and meeting environmental demands

M

MALLEUS MALEFICARUM: A fifteenth century document describing the procedures for identifying and prosecuting witches
MENTAL AGE: (M.A.) level of one's intellectual functioning
MENTAL ILLNESS: General term used to refer to psychological disorders
METHODOLOGY: Approach or way of doing something

MODELING: A form of learning, which involves imitation

MOOD: Characteristic emotional state

MOTIVATION: Drive

MUTUAL RESPECT: Mutuality and respect for others

N

NEGATIVE INFLUENCE: Pressure that hurts and impedes

NEGATIVE REINFORCEMENT: Anything that weakens the strength of a response with which it is associated

NEW TESTAMENT: The second division of the Christian Bible which incorporates the promises of God to man, that are embodied in the life and teachings of Christ

NICENE CREED: A confession of faith for Christians

NORMAL: The value representing the average

NURTURE: Environmental influence on behavior

O

OBSTACLE: Something that makes goal attainment difficult

OLD: Having lived or been in existence for a long period of time

OLD TESTAMENT: The first of the two general divisions of the Christian Bible

OPPOSITE: Against, in contrast with

OPEN: Not shut or blocked up

OPERANT CONDITIONING: A form of learning, that occurs because of reinforcement

P

PARADIGM: A model which illustrates how the psychic system works and deal with thought, perception, feelings and behavior

PARENT SELF-ESTEEM: An individual's perception of his status at home with his parents

PASSAGE: Movement from one place to another

PATHOLOGY: The study of impaired or disordered mental or physical functioning

PATHOLOGICAL: An unhealthy state

PERSEVERE: To persist in spite of obstacles

PERSEVERANCE: To persist in a state, enterprise or undertaking

PERSONA: The mask we present to others; a protective device, to conceal one's true or inner self

PERSONAL: Subjective

PERSONALITY: Characteristics that distinguish one individual from others

PERSONAL SELF-ESTEEM: An individual's most intimate perceptions of self worth

PETITION: A solemn, earnest supplication or request to a superior or deity or to a person or group in authority

POTENTIAL: Ability to act or perform

PRACTICE: To engage in frequently to learn or become proficient

PRAISE: To compliment and congratulate

PRAY: To implore or beseech

PRAYER: The act or practice of praying

PRECEPT: A Commandment or direction meant as a rule of action or conduct

PREJUDICE: A judgment or bias that is likely to cause harm to a person or his or her rights because of the action of others

PROCREATION: The act or process of bringing into being

PROFESSION: A vocation requiring specialized knowledge and often long and intensive academic preparation

PROFICIENT: Highly competent or skilled

PROGNOSIS: Prediction of future outcomes

PROJECTION: Defense mechanism in which the individual rids him or herself of threatening drives, impulses and needs by attributing them to others

PROMINENCE: Center of and distinguished

PROPHET: An interpreter of God's will

PROPHECY: Gift of speaking under the influence of the Holy Spirit

PROPHESY: To declare or predict something by or as by the influence of divine guidance

PSEUDO: Not real, non genuine

PSEUDO LIFESTYLE: One that is incompatible with the morals, principles and values of the experiencing individual

PSEUDO SELF-ESTEEM: Not real, non-authentic perceptions of self-worth

PSYCHOGENIC: Traceable to psychological or environmental experiences

PSYCHOTHERAPY: A general term for psychological treatment procedures

PURPORT: Intended to do

R

RACE: Descendants of a common ancestor

RACE RELATIONS INVENTORY: A self-report inventory that measures racial acceptance and caring

RACISM: The belief that one's own race is superior which often results in antagonism towards members of a different race because of this belief

RACIST: A person who emits racist behavior

RATIONAL: Use of reason as a guide

RATIONAL ECLECTIC APPROACH: A cognitive psychotherapeutic approach, which emphasizes rational thinking

RATIONALIZATION: Defense mechanism in which the individual provides a socially acceptable reason for his undesirable behavior

REACTION FORMATION: Defense mechanism in which an individual feels compelled to react in a fashion that is exactly opposite to how he or she feels

REPRESSION: Defense mechanism in which one removes from conscience and awareness those events that are threatening or anxiety inducing

REPULSION: Strong dislike, distaste or aversion

RESULTS: The outcome of an empirical investigation upon which the conclusion(s) are based

RESURRECTION: To rise again; arising from the dead or coming back to life

S

SABBATH: The day set aside by the commandments to rest and worship

SACRAMENT: A solemn oath or pledge; something regarded as having a sacred character or mysterious meaning

SAINT: A holy person, a righteous, steadfast believer and supporter of God

SALVATION: Deliverance, liberation, saving or being saved

SATAN: The devil, chief of fallen angels

SCAPEGOATING: A form of displacement, which is characterized by the tendency to transfer or displace feelings towards a powerful person, to someone or something else which is considered less threatening

SCRIPTURE: Sacred writing considered to be authoritative and inviolable; writing derived from the teaching of the prophets

SELECTIVE ATTENTION: The tendency to attend to only those aspects of an individual's behavior that is in agreement with one's point of view

SELF-CONFIDENCE: Confidence in oneself and one's powers and abilities

SELF-DEFEATING: Behavior that impedes progress

SELF-DISCLOSURE: The act of opening up; making oneself transparent to others

SELF-ENHANCING: Consequences of behavior that are positive

SELF-ESTEEM: An individual's perception of his or her own worth

SELF-FULFILLING: Brought to fulfillment due to expectation

SELFISH: Egotistic, greedy

SELF-IMAGE: An individual's perception of his or her own traits

SELF-PERPETUATION: Pertaining to the disposition to accentuate and intensify traits that are already present in one-self

SELF-REPORT INVENTORY: An objective checklist or inventory

SHAME: A painful feeling of having lost the respect of others because of the display of behavior

SIN: Moral depravity, transgression or violation of the divine law: break of a religious law or moral principle

SOCIAL PRESSURE: Pressure exerted by others

SOCIAL SELF-ESTEEM: An individual's perception of interpersonal interactions

SOCIAL SKILLS: Skills that promote interpersonal relationships

SOLA FIDA: By faith alone

SOLA GRATIA: By grace alone

SOLA SCRIPTURE: By scripture alone

SOUL: The immortal and spiritual part of individuals

SPIRIT: Soul infused by a deity

SPIRITUAL: Devotional behavior due to belief

STEAL: To take something that belongs to another
STEREOTYPE: A belief about another group that is rigidly established conceptions of the traits that is difficult to change
STRESS: Force applied to a system that taxes the coping strategy of the individual
SUBJECTIVE: Not directly observable by another person but accessible through the individual's own verbal report or introspection
SUCCESS: Achieving desired goals
SUICIDE: A deliberate act of self-injury intended to kill
SUPPLICATION: A humble request or prayer
SUPEREGO: According to intra-psychic or Freudian theorists, the moral aspect of the personality
SYMBOLIZATION: The representation of things by use of symbols
SYMPTOM: A sign or indication of illness
SYNDROME: A group or cluster of symptoms that form a distinctive pathological condition

T

TEACHER: One who teaches
TEMPERAMENT: A constitutional disposition
TEMPT: To try to persuade, induce or entice
TEMPTATION: Being tempted or enticed
TEN COMMANDMENTS: The ten laws constituting the fundamental moral code of Israel
TEST: Any technique for validating or invalidating any hypothesis
TEST BATTERY: A group of tests
TESTEE: Examinee or person being tested
TEST ITEMS: Items that comprise a test
TEST PROFILE: A graphic display of test findings
THEORY: An empirically derived framework of concepts and hypothesized propositions

THERAPY: Generic term that refers to treatment of disorders

TOTAL SELF-ESTEEM: A composite score; for children, derived from general, social, academic and parent facets; for adults, derived from general, social and personal facets

TOXIC PERSON: An individual who impedes the progress of others and exerts negative effects

TRAINEE: One who receives training

TRAINER: One who teaches and prepares others

TRAINING: Act of preparing

TRAIT: An enduring characteristic of an individual

TREPHINATION: Ancient technique of cutting holes in the skull to drive out evil spirits

TRESPASS: To go beyond the limits of what is considered right or moral

U

UNCONSCIOUS: Below the threshold of consciousness

UNCONDITIONAL POSITIVE REGARD: Caring that is not contingent on behavior

V

VAIN: Arrogant, conceited, and egotistical, no real value or significance

VANITY: An act that is empty, worthless, futile

VALIDITY: The extent to which an instrument measures what it purports to measure

VARIABLE: A trait on which events or people differ

VIOLENCE: The act of injuring or directing hostility towards the self, objects, or others

VIRGIN: Chaste, unused

W

WELL-BEING: Well adjusted, happy and content
WICKED: Morbidly bad or wrong behavior with evil intent
WISDOM: Astuteness knowledgeable
WITNESS: An attendant, bystander, testifier
WORK: An achievement, labor, employment
WORKSITE: Place of employment
WORK SKILLS: Skills for employment
WORK TRAINING: Preparation for work
WORSHIP: To honor, dignity, glorify and exalt a deity

Z

ZERO CORRELATION: A lack of association between two distributions

REFERENCES

BATTLE, J. *The North American Depression Inventories For Children and Adults. In Evaluating Stress: A Book of Resources.* Eds. Zalaquett, C. P. and Wood, R. J., Lanham, Md. The Scarecrow Press, Inc. 1997, pp. 219-244

BATTLE, J. *The Anxiety Scales For Children and Adults. In Evaluating Stress: A Book of Resources.* Eds. Zalaquett, C. P. and Wood, R. J. Lanham, Md. The Scarecrow Press, Inc. 1997, pp. 1-22.

BATTLE, J. *Administration And Interpretation of The Culture-Free Self-Esteem Inventories For Children And Adults.* Presentation at the 46th Annual NASAP Convention. Dallas, Texas. May 1998.

BATTLE, J. *Programming For High Risk Youth: A Multifaceted Service Delivery. Model That Promotes Success.* Presentation For National High Risk Youth Initiative. Human Resources Development. Ottawa, Ontario. January 1999.

BATTLE, J. *Programming for High Risk Youth: A Multifaceted Service Delivery Model That Promotes Success. Presentation for Project Officers.* Human Resources Development Alberta Region. February 24, 1999.

BATTLE, J. *Obtaining Goals and Achieving Success: A Workshop For Aboriginal Youth.* Sponsored by the N. W. T. Community Mobilization Agency. Yellowknife, N.W.T., 1999.

BATTLE, J. *A Self-Esteem Skills Development Workshop For Trainers.* Sponsored by the Secretary of State For Children and Youth. RAE Edzo, N.W.T., January, 2000.

BATTLE, J. *A Systematic Program That Promote the Enhancement of Self-Esteem, Literacy And Success At*

Work And In Relationships. A Workshop For Trainers Sponsored by the Secretary of State For Children and Youth. RAE Edzo, N.W.T., January, 2000.

BATTLE, J. *Obtaining Goals and Achieving Success: A Workshop For Youth.* Sponsored by the Secretary of State For Children and Youth. RAE, Edzo, N.W.T., January, 2000.

BATTLE, J. *Obtaining Goals and Achieving Success In Athletics.* Workshop For the Coaches of the Olympian Swim Club. Edmonton, Alberta. March, 2000.

BATTLE, J. *Obtaining Goals and Achieving Success In Athletics.* Workshop For the Parents of the Olympian Swim Club. Edmonton, Alberta. March, 2000.

BATTLE, J. *Obtaining Goals and Achieving Success In Athletics. Workshop For the Athletes of the Olympian Swim Club.* Edmonton, Alberta. March, 2000.

BATTLE, J. *Obtaining Goals And Achieving Success: A Self-Esteem Skills Development Workshop For Youth.* Ft. McPherson Crime Prevention Project Advisory Board and Chief Julius School. October, 2000.

BATTLE, J. *Using Self-Esteem, Mutual Respect And Encouragement to Obtain Goals, Achieve Success And Promote Positive Interactions: A Self-Esteem Skills Development Workshop For Teachers, School Staff and Caregivers.* Ft. McPherson Crime Prevention Project Advisory Board and Chief Julius School. October, 2000.

BATTLE, J. *9 to 19: Crucial Years for Self-Esteem In Children And Youth.* Edmonton: James Battle and Associates Ltd. 1990.

BATTLE, J. *Enhancing Self-Esteem and Achievement.* Edmonton: James Battle and Associates Ltd. 1990.

BATTLE, J. AND WOLOSZYN J. Remediation Strategies For Regular and Special Students. Edmonton: James Battle and Associates Ltd.

BATTLE, J. *Self-Esteem resource book.* Edmonton: James Battle and Associates Ltd. 1990.

BATTLE, J. *Self-Esteem: The New Revolution.* Edmonton: James Battle and Associates Ltd. 1990.

BATTLE, J. *Anxiety Scales For Children And Adults.* Edmonton: James Battle and Associates Ltd. 1992.

BATTLE, J. *Culture-Free Self-Esteem Inventories. 2nd Edition.* Austin: Pro-Ed. 1992.

BATTLE, J. *Enhancing Self-Esteem: A Comprehensive Program of Strategies.* Edmonton: James Battle and Associates Ltd. 1992.

BATTLE, J. *Explanation of Response Choice For The Culture-Free Self-Esteem Inventories.* Edmonton: James Battle and Associates Ltd. 1992.

BATTLE, J. *Instructor's Manual For Self-Esteem, Personality And Adjustment.* Edmonton: James Battle and Associates Ltd. 1992.

BATTLE, J. *Manual For The Culture-Free Self-Esteem Inventories.* Austin: Pro-Ed 1992.

BATTLE, J. *Culture-Free Self-Esteem Inventories, 3rd Edition.* Pro-Ed, 2002.

BATTLE, J. *What You Need To Know About Your Self-Esteem.* Edmonton: James Battle and Associates Ltd. 2002.

BATTLE, J. *Facilitating Self-Sufficiency in Chronic Welfare Recipients.* Workshop For Alberta Social Workers, Southern District, Calgary, Alberta, 1979.

BATTLE, J. *The Self-Esteem of Special Education Students.* Presentation at the Greater Edmonton School Teachers Convention, 1980.

BATTLE, J. *The Effects That A Comprehensive Job Training Program Have On The Self-Esteem Of Young Adults.* Edmonton, Alberta. 1986.

BATTLE, J. *The Effects That A Comprehensive Job Training Program Have On Self-Esteem, Depression And Anxiety Of Young Adults.* Edmonton, Alberta. 1987.

BATTLE, J. *The Effects That A Comprehensive Job Training Program Have On Self-Esteem, Depression And Anxiety Of Young Adults.* Edmonton: James Battle and Associates Ltd. 1989.

BATTLE, J. *Manual For Enhancing Self-Esteem: A Comprehensive Program Of Strategies.* Edmonton: James Battle and Associates Ltd. 1992.

BATTLE, J. *North American Depression Inventories For Children And Adults.* Edmonton: James Battle and Associates Ltd. 1992.

BATTLE, J. *Self-Esteem, Personality And Adjustment.* Edmonton: James Battle and Associates Ltd. 1992.

BATTLE, J. *Self-Esteem Research: A Summary Of Relevant Findings.* Edmonton: James Battle and Associates Ltd. 1992.

BATTLE, J. *Misconceptions Regarding Self-Esteem.* Edmonton: James Battle and Associates Ltd. 1993.

BATTLE, J. *For Teachers, Parents And Kids: Strategies That Enhance Self-Esteem, Achievement And Behavioral Self-Control.* Edmonton: James Battle and Associates Ltd. 1994.

BATTLE, J. *Promoting Self-Esteem, Achievement And Well Being: An Effective Instructional Curriculum For All Levels.* Edmonton: James Battle and Associates Ltd. 1994.

BATTLE, J. *Achieving Success: In Teaching, Parenting, Work And Relationships.* Edmonton: James Battle and Associates Ltd. 1995.

BATTLE, J. *Effective Parenting Tips That Build Self-Esteem.* Edmonton: James Battle and Associates Ltd. 1996.

BATTLE, J. *Self-Esteem Poems.* Edmonton: James Battle and Associates Ltd. 2002.

BATTLE, J. *Strategies That You Can Use To Enhance Your Own Self-Esteem.* Edmonton: James Battle and Associates Ltd. 1996.

BATTLE, J. *Overcoming Racism And Achieving Success.* Edmonton: James Battle and Associates Ltd. 1997.

BATTLE, J. *Peer Exploitation Syndrome: A True Story Of A Teenage Victim.* Edmonton: James Battle and Associates Ltd. 1999.

BATTLE, J. *Dealing With Anger: Strategies That Work.* Edmonton: James Battle and Associates Ltd. 2002.

BATTLE, J. *Interpretation And Treatment Book: A Companion For The Culture-Free Self-Esteem Inventories.* Edmonton: James Battle and Associates Ltd. 2002.

BATTLE, J. *Overcoming Excessive Anxiety, Depression, Low Self-Esteem And Suicidal Ideation.* Edmonton: James Battle and Associates Ltd. 2002.

BATTLE, J. *Explanations For Response Choice, A Guide For The Culture-Free Self-Esteem Inventories.* Edmonton: James Battle and Associates Ltd. 1992.

BATTLE, J. *Enhancing Self-Esteem: A Comprehensive Program Of Strategies.* Edmonton: James Battle and Associates Ltd. 1992.

BATTLE, J. *Tulita Unity Accord.* Tulita N.W.T. February 2007.

BATTLE, J. *Manual For Enhancing Self-Esteem: A Comprehensive Program Of Strategies.* Edmonton: James Battle and Associates Ltd. 1992.

BATTLE, J., SAULNER, F., and CHRISTIAN, J. Reducing The Barriers: An Analysis Of Employment Needs Of Recently Released Federal Offenders. Edmonton: Employment And Immigration And Correctional Service of Canada, 1992.

BRADLEY, D.G. *A Guide to the World Religions. Englewood Cliffs.* M.J.D. Prentice Hale, 1963.

BRANDEN, N. *The Psychology Of Self-Esteem.* New York: Bantam Books, 1969.

BRANDEN, N. *Honoring The Self.* Bantam Books. New York, 1983.

BRANDEN, N. *If You Could Hear What I Cannot Say.* New York, 1983.

BRIGGS, D. C. *Your Child's Self-Esteem.* Garden City, New York. Double Day, 1970.

ELLOR, VERNARD, KIERKE *Good and Radical Discipleship: A New Perspective.* Princeton: Princeton University Press, 1968.

GRITSCH, ERIC *Luther Catechisms of 1529 Whetstones of the church* in Lutheran Theological Seminary Bulletin 60 (1980).

HUTTER, REINHARD *The Ten Commandments- as a Mirror of Sin(s): Anglican Decline Luther Eclipse* in Pro Ecclasia XIV, Winter, 2005.

ILICH, P. *Christianity and The Encounter of World Religions.* New York, Columbia University Press, 1963.

JUNG, C. *Analytical Psychology: Its Theory And Practise.* New York: Vintage Books, 1968.

Catechism of the Catholic Church. New York, Double Day, 1995. Image Books.

KAYER, P. *Prayer, Praise and Thanksgiving.* Lutheran Forum St. Louis, Mo, 2005.

LUTHER, MARTIN *A Life.* Minneapolis, Augsburg, 2003.

LUTHER, MARTIN *Personal Prayer Book.* 1522. Philadelphia, Fortress, 1968.

LUTHER, MARTIN *A Simple Way to Pray.* 1535. Philadelphia, Fortress, 1968.

NESTINGEN, JAMES A. *The Lord's Prayer in Luther's Catechism.* In Word and World 22, Winter 2002.

PANNENBERG, S.O. *The Apostles Creed.* Philadelphia Westminster press 1972.

STEVENSON, D.T. and ROMNEY, D.M. *Depression in learning-disabled children.* Journal of Learning Disabilities 10: 579–582. 1984.

STEVENSON, K.W. *The Lord's Prayer.* Minneapolis, Fortress, 2004.

WHALEN, W.J. AND PFEIFER C.J. *Other Religions In A World of Change.* Ave Maria Press, 1974.

WILKERSON, B. *Mental Health In The Work Place.* Edmonton Journal, 2002.

YANISH, D. and BATTLE, J. *Relationship between Self-Esteem, Depression And Alcohol Consumption Among Adolescents.* Psychological Reports, 57, 331-334. 1985.

YANIW, L. *The Relationship Between Three Affective Variables and Student Achievement.* Unpublished Masters Thesis. Edmonton, Alberta: University of Alberta. 1983.

YEUDALL, L.T. *Clinical Assessment System For Disturbed Adolescents.* Edmonton, Alberta, Alberta Provincial Hospital. 1977.

PART VIII

Recommended Reading and

Resource Materials

RECOMMENDED READING

BOOKS AND PAPERS

BATTLE, J. 1990 *9 To 19: Crucial Years For Self-Esteem In Children and Youth*. Edmonton, AB: James Battle and Associates Ltd.

> In 9 to 19, Dr. Battle identifies characteristics of positive and negative self-esteem, and traces the development of both dispositions. The important role that self-esteem plays in contemporary problems such as learning disabilities, conduct problems, anxiety disorders, depression and suicide is described. In 9 to 19, Dr. Battle offers 110 strategies for remediating these and other problems. The effectiveness of these strategies is documented and actual case reports are provided to illustrate how positive shifts in self-esteem can be induced in students and clients. In the book, Dr. Battle offers concrete ways of identifying problems and acting to correct them, both in the classroom and in the home.

BATTLE, J. 1990 *Enhancing Self-Esteem And Achievement*. Edmonton, AB: James Battle and Associates Ltd.

> The text provides a comprehensive overview of the phenomena that constitute self-esteem. How self-esteem and achievement interacts and supplement each other is clearly delineated, and the author provides empirically tested strategies and techniques that enhance self-esteem and achievement. Twenty-six inventories that assess perception of self worth are described.

BATTLE, J. 1994 *For Teachers, Parents And Kids: Strategies That Promote Self-Esteem, Achievement And*

Behavioral Self-Control. Edmonton, AB: James Battle and Associates Ltd.

In this practical book, Dr. Battle shows teachers, parents and kids how to employ strategies that promote self-esteem, achievement and behavioral self-control. The important role that self-esteem plays in achievement and behavior is delineated and readers are shown how to employ time - tested strategies to enhance the self-esteem and achievement levels of students and assist them in exhibiting behavior that is self-enhancing rather than self-defeating.

BATTLE, J. 2001 *The JBA Model: An Effective Substance Abuse Prevention And Treatment Program.* Edmonton, AB: James Battle and Associates Ltd.

In the JBA Model: An Effective Substance Abuse and Treatment Program, Dr. Battle shows readers how to develop and implement effective substance prevention and treatment programs. In this timely, concisely written book, Dr. Battle, author of the North American Depression Inventories, describe strategies that have demonstrated effectiveness in helping individuals deal with substance use and avoid becoming abusers.

BATTLE, J. 2001 *The JBA Model: An Effective Suicide Prevention Program.* Edmonton, AB: James Battle and Associates Ltd.

In the JBA Model: An Effective Suicide Prevention Program, Dr. Battle shows readers how to develop and implement effective suicide prevention programs. In this concisely written book, Dr. Battle, author of the Culture-Free Self-Esteem Inventories, describe strategies that have demonstrated effectiveness in helping individuals overcome low self-esteem, depression and suicidal ideation.

BATTLE, J. 2001 *Overcoming Excessive Anxiety, Depression, Low Self-Esteem And Suicidal Ideation.* Edmonton, AB: James Battle and Associates Ltd.

In this concise book, Dr. Battle, author of the Culture-Free Self-Esteem Inventories describe time-tested strategies that have demonstrated effectiveness in assisting students, clients and others in overcoming the negative effects of anxiety, depression, low self esteem and suicidal ideation.

BATTLE, J. 1997 *Overcoming Racism and Achieving Success.* Edmonton, AB: James Battle and Associates Ltd.

In Overcoming Racism and Achieving Success, Dr. Battle integrates historical and contemporary observations to show how the problem of racism in North America has persisted. Also, in the text, he shows how perceptions and beliefs promote racist practices at both individual and institutional levels and offers practical strategies that individuals who comprise all groups can use to overcome racism and achieve success.

BATTLE, J. 2003 *What You Need To Know About Your Self-Esteem.* Edmonton, AB: James Battle and Associates Ltd.

In this concisely written book, Dr. Battle author of the first, second, and third editions of The Culture-Free Self-Esteem Inventories offers readers insights that they can use to establish and maintain positive perceptions of self worth. Also, in the text, he describes time-tested practical strategies that have demonstrated effectiveness in helping individuals enhance their self-esteem, obtain goals, and achieve desired levels of success. This book is a must for those experiencing symptoms of low self-esteem such as feelings of worthlessness, pessimism, excessive anxiety, depression, and suicidal ideation.

BATTLE, J. 1990 *Self-Esteem: The New Revolution.* Edmonton, AB: James Battle and Associates Ltd.

In Self-Esteem: The New Revolution, Dr. Battle provides a comprehensive text that addresses the important issue of self-esteem. In the book the author offers 300 strategies that can be used to enhance the self-esteem of individuals at all developmental levels. Empirical data is provided to document the effectiveness of these strategies and actual case reports are presented to illustrate how positive shifts in self-esteem can be induced in individuals of all ages.

BATTLE, J. 1994 *Strategies That You Can Use to Enhance Your Own Self-Esteem and Well Being.* Edmonton, AB: James Battle and Associates Ltd.

In this concise book, Dr. Battle describes strategies that individuals at all stages of development can use to enhance their own self-esteem, achievement and well being. In Strategies That You Can Use to Enhance Your Own Self-Esteem and Well Being, the importance of self-esteem and positive interactions are emphasized and readers are shown how to think and behave in ways that are self-enhancing rather than self-defeating.

BRANDEN, N. 1969 *The Psychology of Self-Esteem.* Los Angeles: Nash Publishing.

The author presents the point of view, which holds that self-esteem is a fundamental human need, and that various levels of self-esteem are consequences of our use of the freedom to think or not to think.

ARTICLES, PRESENTATIONS, AND REPORTS

BATTLE, J. 1993 *Ex-Football Star Preaches Self-Esteem.*

The article states that most problems that students have in school are associated with low self-esteem. It dispels common misconceptions such as low self-esteem is a problem basically of economically disadvantaged individuals and groups.

BATTLE, J. 1991 *No Strings Attached.* Alberta Parents Magazine. March/April.

Common goals of children's misbehavior are identified and parents are shown how to interact with their children and assist them in developing their potential more fully.

BATTLE, J. 1978 *Relationship Between Self-Esteem and Depression.* Psychological Reports 42: 745-746.

Findings confirm the relationship between self-esteem and depression in adults is significant: as depression intensifies, self-esteem diminishes.

Battle, J And Yanish, D.L. 1985 Relationship Between Self-Esteem, Depression, and Alcohol Consumption Among Adolescents. Psychological Reports 57: 331-334.

Findings cited here confirm previous observations which indicate that self-esteem and depression are significantly related: alcohol is associated with the various facets of self-esteem as measured by the Culture-Free Self-Esteem Inventory for Children.

INVENTORIES

BATTLE, J. Culture-Free Self-Esteem Inventories, First and Second Edition

The Culture Free Self-Esteem Inventories are standardized measures of self worth. There are three forms, A, B, are for children and AD is for adults. Forms A and B for children measures children's perceptions of their general self-esteem, (the aspect of self-esteem that refers to individuals overall perceptions regarding self worth). Social self-esteem, (the aspect of self-esteem that refers to individuals perceptions of the quality of their relationships with peers). Academic or school related self-esteem (the aspect of self-esteem that refers to individuals perceptions of their ability to perform academic tasks) and parent/home self-esteem (the aspect of self-esteem that refers to individuals perceptions of their status at home, including their subjective perceptions of how they feel their parents or parent surrogates view them). Form AD measures adult's perceptions of their General self-esteem (the aspect of self-esteem that refers to individuals overall perception of their worth). Social self-esteem (the aspect of self-esteem that refers to individuals perceptions of the quality of their relationships with peers) and Personal self-esteem (the aspect of self-esteem that refers to individuals most intimate perceptions regarding self worth). All forms incorporate a lie facet comprised of items designed to measure defensiveness or the tendency to present oneself in a fashion that is more positive than that which actually exists.

James Battle and Associates Ltd.
1102 10235 124 Street
Edmonton, AB., T5N 1P9

Battle, J. 1992 *North American Depression Inventories*

The North American Depression Inventories are self-report scales which measure symptoms such as sadness, lack of energy, difficulties concentrating, pessimism and suicidal ideation, which indicate the presence of depression. There are two forms, C for children, and A for adults.

James Battle and Associates Ltd.
1102 10235 124 Street
Edmonton, AB., T5N 1P9

BATTLE, J. 1993 *Anxiety Scales*

The Anxiety Scales are self-report inventories that measure symptoms such as nervousness, tenseness, uneasiness, apprehension, and sleep disturbance, which indicate the presence of anxiety. There are two forms, Q for children, and M for adults.

James Battle and Associates Ltd.
1102 10235 124 Street
Edmonton, AB., T5N 1P9

BATTLE, J. 1995 *Mutual Respect Inventories*

The Mutual Respect Inventories are self-report scales with a response continuum ranging from always to never, which measures how individuals communicate with others and the level of respect they provide while interacting with them. There are many forms including scales for adults, children, parents, teachers, social workers, youth workers, spouses, athletes, coaches and service providers.

James Battle and Associates Ltd.
1102 10235 124 Street
Edmonton, AB., T5N 1P9

BATTLE, J. 1996 *Encouragement Inventories*

The Encouragement Inventories are self-report scales with a response continuum ranging from always to never, which measures how individuals communicate with others and the level of encouragement they provide while interacting with them. There are many forms including scales for adults, children, parents, teachers, social workers, youth workers, spouses, athletes and coaches.

James Battle and Associates Ltd.
1102 10235 124 Street
Edmonton, AB., T5N 1P9

BATTLE, J. 2003 *Culture-Free Self-Esteem Inventories, Third Edition*

The Culture-Free Self-Esteem Inventories are standardized measures of self worth. There are three Forms, Primary for Children aged 6 to 8 years; Intermediate Form, for Children aged 9 to 12 years and Adolescent Form, for Youth aged 13 to 18 years. The Primary Form measures children's perceptions of their academic or school related self-esteem (the aspect of self-esteem that refers to individuals perceptions of their ability to perform academic tasks);general self-esteem(the aspect of self-esteem that refers to individuals overall perceptions of self worth), parent / home self-esteem (the aspect of self-esteem that refers to individuals perceptions of their status at home, including their subjective perceptions of how they feel their parents or parent surrogates view them), and social self-esteem, (the aspect of self-esteem that refers to individuals perceptions of the quality of their relationships with peers). The Intermediate Form is comprised of the same four facets (academic, general, parental, home and social) incorporated in the Primary and Adolescent Forms; however, in addition to these, the Adolescent Form also incorporate items that measure personal self-esteem, (the aspect of self-esteem that refers to individuals most intimate perceptions regarding self worth). All Forms incorporate a lie facet comprised of items designed to measure defensiveness or the tendency to present oneself in a fashion that is more positive than that which actually exists.

James Battle and Associates Ltd.
1102 10235 124 Street
Edmonton, AB., T5N 1P9

POEMS

BATTLE, J. 1992 *Poems. (The complete set of poems include):*

1. The Self-Esteem Poem

2. Children: Important Resources

3. Children: You and Me

4. My Mom and Dad

5. Then I Reflected and Thanked My God

6. Show Them

7. My Favorite Teacher

8. Anger

9. Gramma

10. My Wife

11. Remembrance

12. My Greatest Asset

James Battle and Associates Ltd.
1102 10235-124 Street
Edmonton, AB., T5N 1P9

PROGRAM

BATTLE J. 1992 *Enhancing Self-Esteem: A Comprehensive Program of Strategies*

James Battle and Associates Ltd.
1102 10235-124 Street
Edmonton, AB., T5N 1P9

TAPES AND CD'S

BATTLE, J. 1990 *Strategies you Can Use to Enhance Your Own Self-Esteem And Well Being*

James Battle and Associates Ltd.
1102 10235-124 Street
Edmonton, AB., T5N 1P9

BATTLE, J. 1990 *Effective Parenting Tips That Build Self-Esteem, Revised*

James Battle and Associates Ltd.
1102 10235-124 Street
Edmonton, AB., T5N 1P9

VIDEO / VHS–DVD

BATTLE, J. 1992 *Enhancing Self-Esteem: A Comprehensive Program Of Strategies*

James Battle and Associates Ltd.
1102 10235-124 Street
Edmonton, AB., T5N 1P9

PART IX

Epilogue

Doing God's Will: Using Christian Faith and
Psychology

This manuscript is a faith based, God inspired book
that provides effective knowledge intended to promote
mutual respect, peace and harmony among all peoples.
A variety of interventions spanning the years 2003 to 2007
resulted in the development, writing and publication of
`Doing God's Will: Using Christian Faith and
Psychology' these include:

1. Having the national bishop of the Christian
denomination that I am a member of visit with me and
my wife at our home.

2. Discussing the need for Christians to strive to
become authentic with the national bishop of my
religious denomination.

3. Discussing the needs with the national bishop for
bishops to receive instruction regarding the relationship
between the Christian faith and psychology.

4. Making lesson plans and instructional overheads to
serve as teaching tools for Synod Bishops if the
opportunity occurred.

5. Becoming aware of the diagnosis of stomach cancer
in my 83 year old mother-in-law, who was considered to
be in excellent health by most people who knew her.

6. Having my mother-in-law proof read the
overheads I developed as teaching aids, when she was
hospitalized in efforts to encourage her to fight to live.

7. Making the decision to write the book entitled
`Doing God's Will: Using Christian Faith and
Psychology'.

8. Having three Christian friends volunteer to
conduct searches of the Christian bible.

9. Having a Christian staff member employed by my wife and I volunteer to type the book.

10. Having a Christian who worked with the team that printed several of my earlier publications volunteer to type set the book.

11. Having a graduate of the employment training program that my wife and I have facilitated for more than 20 years win a lottery prize of 8.8 million dollars and using this gift to do God's will by serving others.

The information recorded in this section make it clear to me that this book is inspired by God and a consequence of him working within me. God made it clear to me that … **It will work out…**

With mutual respect

And

God Bless

Dr. James Battle, Ph.D. R. Psych